Missing Lauren and Other Stories

Megan Fairchild

Published by Trellis Publishing, 2021.

MISSING LAUREN AND OTHER STORIES

First edition. July 4, 2021.

ISBN: 979-8224039876

Written by Megan Fairchild.

MISSING LAUREN AND OTHER STORIES

1

MEGAN FAIRCHILD

The Unsolved Disappearance of Lauren Spierer

Lauren Spierer was a 20-year college student at Indiana University at the time of her disappearance in June 2011. Her disappearance, subsequent police manhunt and investigation, generated widespread coverage in the national news. There has been tons of speculation and gossip as to what happened that night and the notable reluctance of the Bloomington Police Department to release further footage of the surveillance cameras of her walking outside the bar. But what remains most haunting about the case is Lauren herself. A bright and beautiful young woman, her smile captured the hearts of everyone who met her and everyone who saw her face on her missing posters. Lauren's Spierer's disappearance remains one of the most well-known unsolved mysteries in modern U.S. History.

This is what happened that night...

Who Was Lauren Spierer?

Lauren Spierer was born in Scarsdale, New York in January 1991 to Robert Spierer and Charlene Spierer. She was raised in the Scarsdale, a small town of just over 17,000 people, located in Westchester County and a short train ride from New York City.

"In all of her family videos," forensic psychologist Paul Jones said. "Lauren is shown to be a vivacious young lady with a zest for life. She sings and dances and mugs for the camera. She obviously came from a loving home."

Lauren would graduate from Edgemont High School in 2009 and moved to Indiana that year to begin studying for a bachelor's degree in textiles and merchandising.

Spierer enrolled at Indiana University along with a close circle of friends and her boyfriend, Jesse Wolff. Lauren met Jesse during her childhood at Camp Towanda, a summer camp for teenagers in Pennsylvania. While Lauren was a strong student, she was arrested for public intoxication roughly nine months before she disappeared.

"I don't think I realized to what degree, you know?" Lauren's mother said. "It was a little bit of a shock."

Shortly after completing her finals in the spring semester of her sophomore year, Lauren went out for a night of partying with friends. She would never be seen again.

The Night of the Disappearance

Lauren set out to her friend's house on the night of June 3rd, 2011 for a night of partying at a local sports bar. She left her apartment at the Smallwood Plaza apartment complex with her friend David Rohn, traveling to their mutual friend Jay Rosenbaum's house before heading out to the bar. While at Rosenbaum's house, Spierer and Rohn begin drinking and "pre-gaming" with Rosenbaum's neighbor, Cory Rossman. The three students spent nearly an hour drinking before heading to Kilroy's Sports Bar shortly after 1:30am.

"Kilroy's was 'the' hangout near the campus," Jones said. "It was a crowded place not only inside but outside as well with tons of college students just milling about. It would be easy to get lost in the shuffle with all the people that are there. Too easy for a predator, if there was one, to target a victim and wait for her to separate from the pack."

Witnesses who were present at the bar describe Lauren and her friends as very intoxicated and she is reported as having fallen down several times while out partying. The friends spent a little less than hour at the sports bar before Lauren and Rossman are spotted leaving the bar and heading to her apartment complex. Lauren's shoes and cell phone are later found at the bar, and she is seen walking barefoot down the street, heavily intoxicated, by a concerned passerby.

Surveillance cameras would show Lauren entering her apartment complex minutes after leaving the nearby sports bar, but she would be seen leaving her apartment and stumbling into a nearby alley minutes after.

Brad Garrett, a former FBI agent who assisted 20/20 with their investigation into Lauren's disappearance claims that Rossman got into a physical confrontation with several of her neighbors, leading to their departure from her apartment complex. Garrett said, "Apparently they don't like the way [Rossman] is handling Lauren. And Rossman supposedly said something smart to him and this guy decides to deck him."

She and Rossman then walked over to Rossman's apartment, where Rossman vomited on his way up the stairs. Rossman's roommate, Michael Beth, would later report that both friends were visibly intoxicated, stumbling and slurring their words. Beth soon helped Rossman get to bed and offered Lauren a place to stay for the night. Lauren declined and headed next door to her close friend Jay Rosenbaum's apartment before heading back to her apartment. She was last seen walking south on College Avenue, near the intersection of College Avenue and 11th Street.

Later that morning, Lauren's boyfriend, Jesse Wolff, texted Lauren to ask how she was doing. After receiving a reply from a staff member of Kilroy's Sports Bar stating that her phone was left at the bar, Wolff reported her as missing to the local police department.

Police Timeline

12:30am – Spierer is spotted leaving her apartment with her close friend David Rohn. The two meet up with Cory Rossman, the neighbor of their mutual friend Jay Rosenbaum.

1:46am – Spierer is spotted entering Kilroy's Sports Bar. It is later reported that Spierer used a fake ID to get into the bar.

2:37am – Witnesses see Lauren leave the sports bar with Cory Rossman. Spierer left her shoes and cell phone at the bar. The pair set off to Spierer's apartment.

2:30am – Witnesses see Spierer enter her apartment complex, Smallwood Plaza. A man named Zach Oakes, whiling walking past Spierer, notices that she is severely intoxicated and asks if she is "okay."

2:48am – Spierer is spotted by security cameras leaving her apartment and entering an alley located between College Avenue and

Morton Street. She did not enter her apartment or put a new pair of shoes on.

2:51am – Security cameras capture Lauren and Rossman leaving the alley and walking towards an empty parking lot. Police would later find Spierer's keys and wallet lying on the ground in the vicinity of her path.

3:00am – Lauren and Rossman arrive at Rossman's apartment. Rossman's roommate, Michael Beth, reported that both friends were heavily intoxicated and having difficulties walking. Rossman was spotted vomiting on the way upstairs. Beth reported that he helped Rossman to bed and encouraged Spierer to spend the night until she could sober up, but Spierer declined.

3:30am – Beth called his neighbor and Spierer's friend Jay Rosenbaum to enlist his help in taking care of Spierer. Lauren goes to Rosenbaum's apartment and used his phone to place two calls before leaving his apartment.

3:38am – A local bar manager later says that he saw a man pick up a woman matching Lauren's description and sling her over his shoulder near 10th Street and College Avenue. There is no video evidence to support this assertion, but a private investigator hired by the Spierer's later says that he believes this was Lauren, but that the bar manager's recollection of the time this happened was incorrect.

4:30am – Rosenbaum states that Lauren left his apartment, purportedly to return to her own apartment. He states that he last saw her walking south along College Avenue, near the corner of College Avenue and 11th Street. She was described as wearing black leggings and a white shirt, and barefoot.

4:35am – There are reports that a homeless man hears a woman scream for help near where Spierer was last seen. Investigators have been unable to confirm this rumor, but a local homeless man, Franklin "Road Dog" Crawford, who may have been the man in question died just days after Lauren's disappearance.

4:30pm – Friends of Lauren report her as missing to the local Bloomington Police Department. Lauren's sister, Rebecca, calls Robert and Charlene Spierer to tell them that Lauren has been reported as missing. They call Lauren's boyfriend, Jesse Wolff, who is at the Bloomington police station when he receives the call.

Police Investigation

Police conducted a nine-day search of the areas near her apartment, including the Sycamore Ridge Landfill located in Pimento, Indiana. They were joined by Lauren's parents, the Bloomington Police Department, the Indiana University Police Department, FBI, and hundreds of volunteers, searching the abandoned landfill, local forests, and quarries. However, their extensive search would ultimately prove fruitless. Although the authorities received hundreds of tips related to her disappearance, none of the leads led to any answers.

"The search would be an emotionally brutal time for Lauren's parents," Jones said. "They would have to go through the agony of walking through creeks and quarries shouting out their daughter's name to no avail. The father said that the worst time was when they witnessed the city bulldozer sift through the nearby landfill. Combing through the garbage, looking for their daughter. The pain they experienced is simply unimaginable."

Drug Use the Night of the Disappearance

Former FBI investigator and 20/20 researcher Brad Garrett has stated that he believes drugs played a part in her disappearance that night, stating that they had role "either in her own demise or because it placed her in harm's way because she was so impaired." In addition, both Lauren's boyfriend and her friends told police officers that she used both drugs and alcohol on a regular basis leading up to her disappearance. Officers would later find "a small amount of cocaine" during a search of her apartment and Lauren's parents would later reveal that she was arrested for public intoxication and underage consumption of alcohol approximately nine months before her disappearance.

Nadine Wolff, the mother of Lauren's boyfriend Jesse Wolff, would later claim that Lauren was kicked out of the summer camp where she met Jesse and her core group of friends in high school because of drug use.

"This poor little girl is not with us today because of her drug abuse," Nadine said.

For their part, Lauren's parents would later respond in the press that "We are appalled that the Wolff's have defamed our daughter knowing that Lauren will never have the opportunity to respond."

Rosenbaum would corroborate these claims of drug use that night, telling authorities that Lauren snorted Klonopin and cocaine that evening, in addition to drinking a large amount of alcohol. Her family would also disclose that Lauren suffered from a rare heart condition, long QT syndrome, which may have been a contributing factor.

While police have stated that this may be a case of her friends disposing of her body to hide her overdose in their presence, they have also stated that this may be a case of abduction. A private investigator later hired by the Spierer's would similarly express doubt that this may have simply been a case of students panicking after Lauren suffered an overdose.

Parents' Public Statements

Lauren's parents have publicly said that they believe Lauren is dead. Robert Spierer has speculated that, given Lauren's erratic behavior the night of her disappearance and extreme level of intoxication, she may have been drugged while at the bar.

"One of her friends stated that it wouldn't be out of the ordinary for her to take off her shoes at the bar," Jones said. "They would have beach sand inside the bar to add to the party atmosphere. As far as leaving her cell phone there, she may have just been completely out of it and forgot it."

Lauren's parents have also stated that they believe the young men Lauren partied with that night, and possibly her boyfriend, know more about her disappearance than they have let on. They base these accusations on the fact that all of the men involved refused to take a polygraph test and hired lawyers shortly after Lauren's disappearance.

Suspects

Her Group of Friends

Brad Garrett, the former FBI agent hired by Lauren's parents to investigate her disappearance, stated that the first suspects in her disappearance were her friends. He said, "When something happens to someone, it's usually from their own circle." Robert Spierer, Lauren's father, has noted on several occasions that the young men with Lauren the night of her disappearance, sought legal representation "very early on," which he claims created a "wall of access" that prevented the family from learning more about their daughter's last hours.

In addition, while Lauren's boyfriend, Jesse Wolff, was very helpful in the beginning of the investigation and cooperated fully with the police, her father notes that Wolff's parents brought him home to New York shortly after Lauren's disappearance, saying "I thought it was odd." It should be noted that Wolff was never spotted outside of his apartment the night of Lauren's disappearance, and he says that he was at home watching the NBA finals while she was out drinking. Wolff's roommate says that Wolff was in bed by 2:30am, hours before Lauren was last seen.

Despite Wolff's alibi and statements from Lauren's friends describing Wolff as "the most loving boyfriend" who would never harm Lauren, the Spierer's are still unsure of Wolff's potential involvement. Brad Garrett told 20/20 that he's "not comfortable that [he] actually knows what he was doing in the early morning hours of June 3."

Cory Rossman, who had only recently met Lauren and spent most of the night with her the night of her disappearance, provided a DNA sample to the police early in their investigation and has maintained his innocence. However, Rossman has refused to speak with the Spierers or their private investigators, claiming to have lost his memory after being punched in Lauren's apartment complex. Robert Spierer has noted that he is skeptical of Rossman's statements, saying "I'm not sure of anything, but what I do know is that there's been a complete lack of cooperation. And he was the person who spent the most time with Lauren in the last hours of her being seen."

While Rossman seldom speaks with reporters about the case, he told the press in 2011 that "I was not the last person with her and that's all I can say, I'm sorry. But I just hope they find her as soon as possible and I am praying for her and her family."

"If we're to judge who looks the most suspicious," Jones said. "My bet is on Rossman. His mug shot is certainly suggestive of someone who is angry and secretive. Out of all the persons of interests he has behaved as if he is either guilty or knows a lot more than he has revealed."

The White Pickup Truck

Another well-known scenario is that Lauren was abducted by a stranger who was driving around Bloomington the night of her disappearance, and who may have viewed a visibly intoxicated, stumbling, and shoeless Lauren as an ideal target. Police have stated that surveillance footage from nearby businesses show a white pickup truck driving around the area where Lauren was last seen. A local police official would say that it is "absolutely" possible that this truck may have been involved in Lauren's disappearance.

Brad Garrett, the investigator hired by Lauren's parents, has theorized that James McClish, a felon was recently released from prison at the time of Lauren's disappearance, may have been involved. He was released from prison after being convicted of assaulting his ex-wife and reportedly drove a white pickup truck at this time. He was living in a halfway house for recently released convicts just minutes away from where Lauren was last seen. Garrett says that her abduction "could have taken 10 seconds. At that point he's got her and he takes her to wherever."

During the course of Garrett's investigation, he says that a woman who knew McClish telephoned him and told him, "You need to check him out. He was there. He's made comments, 'You know what happened to her [Lauren], the same thing could happen to you." She also claimed that McClish murdered Lauren and buried her body on a farm.

However, McClish was approached about this claim by 20/20 and he agreed to take a lie detector test, administered by a former NYPD detective and polygraph examiner, Ralph Nieves. After administering the test, Nieves said that McClish was telling the truth and was not involved in Lauren's disappearance. After finishing the test, McClish told the investigators "I wish you guys the best of luck. I do."

A Lead from Jail

In 2012, another student at Indiana University, Corey Hamersley, was arrested after suffering a mental breakdown while high on drugs and after shooting at local police officers. Hamersley was reportedly heavily involved in the drug culture at Indiana University and was a former star athlete for the university.

Shortly after being sentenced to 24 years in prison for firing at police officers, an inmate in the same cell block as Hamersley claims that Hamersley said of Lauren's disappearance, "I knew the guy that did that."

"This is one of those jailhouse confessions," Jones said. "We really don't know if it has credibility or not but the inmate stated that Hamersley told him that Lauren overdosed on ecstasy. She passed out and they didn't know what to do with her so they drove her down to the Ohio River and dumped her body there. Far fetched for any normal human being to do something like that. The normal response would be to call 911. But these are drunk college students from privileged backgrounds. They do not want anything on their record that would mar their futures."

Brad Garrett says he believes that there could be some truth to this story, "Because the idea is very simple. One of the mistakes in most criminal cases is we, investigators, try to make them too complicated... The simplest is, she dies at a party in Bloomington and somebody got rid of her." This theory on Lauren's disappearance is even more compelling when you consider that Lauren suffered from a heart condition that could have led to an overdose or adverse reaction.

For his part, Hamersley denies any involvement in Lauren's disappearance, and has stated "absolutely" did not help move her body, and that "I do not want to be associated with this at all."

Civil Lawsuit

Robert and Charlene Spierer filed a civil lawsuit against the three young men who were with Lauren the night of her disappearance, Cory Rossman, Jay Rosenbaum, and Michael Beth. Lauren's parents claimed that the three men were negligent in their care of Lauren the night of her disappearance, and that both Rossman and Rosenbaum provided Lauren with alcohol throughout the night despite the fact that she was "visibly intoxicated."

Despite the fact that none of the men have been publicly named as suspects by the local police department, Charlene Spierer publicly said, "I truly don't think it was a random abduction, I think that somebody Lauren knew was responsible for the events of that evening."

Eventually, the civil lawsuit against each of the young men would be dismissed. In their suit against Michael Beth, Robert and Lauren Spierer claimed that he had assumed a "duty of care" for Lauren when she arrived at his apartment visibly intoxicated and he offered to allow her to stay the night. The federal judge presiding over the case, Tanya Pratt, dismissed the case against Beth in 2013, saying that he had no duty to care for Lauren Spierer, despite her level of intoxication.

Judge Pratt would then dismiss the Spierer's case against Cory Rossman and Jay Rosenbaum in 2014, saying that, "Unfortunately, there could be any number of theories as to what happened to Lauren and what, if any, injuries she may have sustained. Without evidence to provide these theories, it would be impossible for a jury to determine if whatever happened to Spierer was a natural and probable cause of her intoxication, without any other intervening acts that would break the causal chain."

Robert and Charlene Spierer maintain that the three young men were involved in the disappearance of Lauren and have appealed the dismissal of their civil suits. They have also hired private investigators to look into the three men's possible role in their daughter's disappearance, and have publicly claimed that the men have been less than cooperative with the family and the police throughout the process. Ron Chapman, the attorney for Michael Beth and David Rohn, countered, "They've been interviewed and interviewed and interviewed, and to say they've been less than forthcoming is just not accurate."

Recent Developments

The Bloomington Police Department publicly stated that Lauren's disappearance may be related to the abduction and murder of another IU student, Hannah Wilson. Wilson was also partying at Kilroy's Sports Bar the night of her disappearance on April 24, 2015, before leaving the bar in a taxi.

Wilson's body was found the next day in Brown County, Indiana, and her murder was investigated as a possible link to Spierer's case. However, despite the arrest of a local man, Daniel Messel, in Wilson's murder, a private investigator hired by the Spierer's determined that the two cases were unrelated.

In January 2016, the FBI and local police department began to investigate a property belonging to the family of Justin Wagers, a registered sex offender, who police believe may have been involved in Lauren's disappearance.

"Wagers was a serial flasher," Jones said. "He'd yell 'Hey Lady!' at women and expose himself, getting arrested numerous times. His behavior did escalate, however, and he did work for an excavation company so he would know how to hide a body. But his involvement is pure speculation. For the most part, flashers are different animals than a kidnapping rapist."

The house, located in the 2900 block of Old Morgantown Road in Martinsville, Indiana, was searched by officers with cadaver dogs. The dogs got a "hit" on the site, which caused a team of forensic investigators to dig up parts of the property in search of evidence related to Lauren's disappearance, but no definitive evidence was found.

Lauren's case remains open and although the case has been "reinvigorated" the mystery of her disappearance seems no more closer to being solved than the night she vanished.

MISTY COPSEY

LORI DUNLAP

Misty Copsey was fourteen years old when she disappeared on September 17th, 1992 after a trip to the Puyallup Fair.

Her case remains a showcase of administrative screw-ups and dropped balls. She was initially thought of as a runaway before foul play was finally suspected a month after the fact. Subsequently, there have been at least five people suspected of committing her abduction.

But the Puyallup police did not get within sniffing distance of Misty or charging anyone with her disappearance. Three different police chiefs and numerous detectives all took a swing at the case and whiffed. No one in law enforcement has been able to answer the question on everyone's lips.

What happened to Misty Copsey?

A GOOD GIRL

Misty was born in 1978 to Diana and Paul "Buck" Copsey. Her father was a firefighter but the couple split up shortly after she was born and Misty lived with her mother.

Misty got good grades in school, excelling particularly in Math. During her last quarter at Spanaway Lake Junior High School, she got A's and B's. Athletic, she played softball, volleyball, and basketball before breaking both forearms during an athletic practice.

Misty was not the ringleader of a bad crowd. She was diffident but funny, entertaining her friends while skipping around and singing the theme song to Sesame Street.

She did not have much in regards to material wants. Her mother eked out a living as an in-home care nurse and they lived in a mobile home park until she was fourteen. Seeking a better place to live, Diana and Misty moved into a duplex where she now had her own room. But Misty longed for her friend who lived in and around the old trailer park. She would make it back there when she could to just hang out.

Tall, blonde and with green eyes, Misty was cute enough to draw the attention of boys. She remained chaste, however, and was not dating like so many of her other friends.

Her innocent, girl-next-door looks would draw the attention of Rheuban Schmidt. Rheuban looked like a casting call actor for a meth head. He sported a reverse mullet, a hairstyle that was cut close to the sides with curls on top. He had beady, green eyes that screamed low IQ. One of Misty's friends described him as a "scuzzy looking dude" but he nonetheless befriends Misty, much to the chagrin of her mother.

Diana grew suspicious of the relationship as Rheuban was four years older and a high school dropout. On one occasion, she listened in on the other end of a phone conversation Misty was having with Rheuban.

"I get horny just looking at you, Misty," Rheuban said, whispering like an old pervert.

Diana became enraged and ordered her daughter off the phone.

"Don't ever talk to that idiot again...."

ENTER CORY BOBER

Cory Bober was a thorn in the side of police every since the Green River killings became a national news story. He would insist that the police are "incompetent fools" while organizing his own searches for her remains. Diana would later accuse him of killing her daughter but he would respond by telling Diana that she was being "ungrateful." He was, after all, the only man on the case.

Bober was a recluse without a vehicle or a drive's license. An inveterate marijuana user, he had a record for both possession and dealing. He was also obsessed with cases of murdered or slain women in his home state of Washington. He had a stack of binders with autopsy reports, pictures, and other arcane details.

Bober came under the radar of the police in Puyallup when he became obsessed with the Green River Killer case. He had a brief acquaintance with Randall Dean Achziger, remembering a conversation where the man told him that the killer inserted rocks into the remains of his victim. Bober became suspicious as that would turn out to be a piece of information only known to police. He then went on a one-man crusade to prove the guilt of Achziger. Bober would interview his ex-girlfriends, friends, co-workers and present all of this in an affidavit to the courts.

Achziger found it ridiculous and annoying.

So did the police.

The Green River Killer would turn out to be a painter named Gary Leon Ridgway.

Bober didn't give up, however. He knew Achziger was the guy.

Bober had his own theories about who was performing the killings. Some were wild and outlandish conspiracy theories. Others were spot on. He would notice that there were victims that "had disappeared on the very same date that others were discovered. Some victims seemed to almost 'commemorate' the deaths or discoveries of others; one would die on a particular date and another would disappear a year to the day later on the very same date."

The police dismissed his theories as the rantings of a crack head. But Bober would be willing to show the proof of his connect the dots calculations. He pointed to the cases of Kim Delange, a 15-year-old killed in 1988 and Anna Chebetnoy, a 14-year-old killed in 1990. Both of their bodies would be found along Highway 410, east of Enumclaw.

Bober discovered that the remains of both girls were found in the same section of 410. The girls were found two years and one month apart. He felt that the killer was following a pattern.

He called the police department and left a voice mail. He predicted that a teen girl from Puyallup would disappear and her remains would be found on Highway 410 in the same vicinity where the other girl's bodies were found. Bober gave him the name of the man whom he felt was the serial killer.

Randall Achziger.

But the police were now used to his calls and viewed him as a crank. A nutcake with a strange vendetta.

His prediction would be half-right, however.

There would be no body found on Highway 410.

But a teenage girl would disappear.

Her name was Misty Copsey.

A NIGHT AT THE FAIR

On September 17th, 1992, Diana told her daughter Misty and her best friend Trina Bevard to behave themselves. Misty had convinced her mother to let them stay out that night...free of any meddlesome adults. But Trina's guardian would not allow her to go without an adult driving them home.

Diana worked as a caregiver for a 97-year-old Alzheimer patient who could not be left alone. She would not be able to drive the girls home. But Misty checked the bus schedules and convinced her mother that they would be okay. There was a bus that left the fair at 8:40 p.m.

Misty then convinced her mother to lie to Trina's guardian, Marlene Shoemaker.

"No worries," Diana said to Marlene. "I'll bring them home."

She wanted to be the cool parent, different from the stuffy adults who forgot what it was like to be fourteen. If it meant telling a white lie so her little girl could have some happiness, so be it.

What was the worst that could happen?

Diana dropped the girls off and gave them one last warning.

"Get home safe."

It would be the last time she would ever see her daughter again.

THE PHONE CALL

A few hours later, Diana would then receive a phone call from Misty as she tended to her elderly patient. Misty told her that she had missed the bus but could get a ride from Rheuban Schmidt.

Diana, knowing what kind of unsavory character Schmidt was, adamantly refused. She told Misty to find someone else to give her a ride back. Misty had an electronic diary which she used to store phone numbers. She told her mother she would find someone trustworthy to call for a ride.

"You call me back when you find someone," Diana said.

"I will. I promise."

Diana would wait all night for the phone call.

In the ensuing hours, Misty would not call back.

Worried, Diane called home in the hope that Misty had gotten a ride without calling her.

No answer.

Diana didn't panic. She figured that Misty went home with that scumbag Schmidt and didn't want to get yelled out for disobeying her.

She's going to get yelled at either/or. All Diana wanted was for her daughter to be safe.

Her shift finally ended and Diana drove back home in a rush.

Upon entering her house, she called out for Misty.

Silence.

She went into Misty's room and saw that it had been untouched from the previous night.

Diana would call the police in a panic. She told them that her daughter had not come home from the fair. The dispatcher would tell her that the police could not do anything about it for thirty days as it "sounded like a runaway case."

Diana knew otherwise.

Trying to calm herself, she figured that Misty was with Trina, that the two of them would be okay.

She called Trina's home.

No answer.

She then began scorching the earth with phone calls.

She would call Rheuban but he told her that she called but he didn't have the gas to go get her. She then called numerous friends of Misty and her mother.

No one had seen Misty.

She called Trina's home again, got no answer, then drove out to her house. She then went to the police department and filed a formal report with the Pierce County's Sheriff's Department who handled runaways as opposed to the Puyallup Police.

MISTY'S MISSING

Misty's friend Trina called Diana after she came back from school. She told the frantic mother that she didn't know where Misty was.

"The last time I saw her, she was heading for the bus," she said.

Diana would call Rheuban again. She would get his roommate this time, James Tinsley.

Diana needed answers. She interrogated the young fifteen-year-old like a grizzled police detective. She asked if Rheuban had been home all night. James then told her that Rheuban and his uncle went to pick up Misty but that he wasn't home just yet.

Later, Diana would call back and Rheuban would tell her that his roommate got the story wrong. He went to a party instead and didn't pick up Misty. He didn't know where she was.

Diana pleaded for the police to do something. They dragged their heels and began talking to some of Misty's friends. "Just call if she calls," they informed them. "No one gets in trouble."

Diana printed fliers with Misty's picture. She plastered them in and around the fairgrounds while calling the media.

The one woman search team would yield no leads. Rheuban would stop by and ask if the police had found anything yet. Diana would then wait at the bus stop near the fairgrounds to inquire with different drivers on the route. She found one driver who said that he saw Misty. She had asked when the next bus to Spanaway was arriving. The driver said it wasn't and that he was done for the night. He gave her instructions on which bus to take but she walked away before he could complete his sentence.

AN ERROR OF JUDGEMENT

Among the many mistakes that the Puyallup police made in the investigation of Misty's disappearance was to make the assumption that she was a runaway. Why they didn't entertain the prospect that she could have been kidnapped and murdered gave the abductor precious time to cover his tracks.

The police came to this erroneous conclusion after they interviewed Misty's mother, Diana. They thought she was a liar and an alcoholic. They then interviewed a pair of Misty's classmates who really didn't know her that well or accompany her to the fair.

A series of cover-ups then ensued, as the police told the media Misty had been found (where they got that information remains a mystery) and made no further investigation.

Until Diana and the media started to make a fuss. The department had to save face and eventually one of the detectives believed that this was not a runaway case.

Misty's disappearance could not be ignored any longer.

Police would talk to the various fair workers and security guards. No one had recalled seeing Misty.

The police then turned to her family, interviewing and doing background checks on both Misty's father, Buck, and Diana.

Their impressions of the duo would support their initial theory that Misty runaway. Diana was an alcoholic with multiple DUIs and seven years prior she had been convicted of welfare fraud. Buck confirmed that his daughter and Diana would have their issues.

Carver then discovered that Diana had filed a runaway report on Misty a month prior to her disappearing.

Diana would later state that the report was wrong. She thought Misty had disappeared then found her in the bedroom. She was too ashamed to tell the police it had been a false alarm.

With the police questioning and media coverage, Misty Copsey was now the talk of her Spanaway Lake Junior High school.

Rumors would abound at the school, one of which came from Misty Matthews who said that Misty had called her from Olympia. Another student stated that she saw Misty at a Color Me Badd concert at the fair.

The rumors were enough to prompt Carver to remove Misty from the FBI's National Crime Information Center as a missing person. He would once again treat her as a runaway.

BOBER'S THEORY

Cory Bober's knew he was right. He knew that police would find a body of a young woman off Highway 410.

He waited but nothing happened.

Until his mother showed him the flier of Misty's disappearance.

Right again!

Heart racing, he called the number on the flier. Bober would get into contact with Diana and hurriedly told her all about his research.

He talked about the Green River Killer, where and how he killed his victims. He would tell Diana that her disappearance was connected to the same guy responsible for the murdered Puyallup Girls, Kim Delange and Anne Chebetnoy.

Cory would apologize to Diana because he knew that Misty was dead. He predicted her body would be found somewhere along Highway 410.

The two would form an uneasy alliance. Bober became Misty's personal avenger. He would start a phone/letter/media campaign to prove the police wrong and himself right.

Misty was no runaway.

She was a victim of Randall Achziger.

In October, however, Bober would be arrested for selling marijuana. He was then accosted by Sgt.Herm Carver who tired of the young man meddling in police affairs.

"He walked in the room I was being held in – looking tired and pissed off. He said, 'I got out of bed tonight, and came down here to meet you – just to see what kind of a hypocrite you REALLY ARE!'

I said (being cocky), 'It's not MY FAULT – HERM – that you don't believe Misty Copsey's MISSING!!'

He yelled (angry), 'DON'T YOU EVER CALL ME BY MY FIRST NAME – IT'S SGT. CARVER TO YOU!!!'"

Bober's journals, November 1992

THIRTY DAYS MISSING

Sgt. Herm Carver and Deputy Brian Coburn would each individually warn Diana of the troublemaker that Bober was. Still, the worried mother would welcome his assistance as she needed all the help she could get. After numerous phone calls, the two would finally meet after a month of Misty being missing. Diana had nowhere else to turn but to the shaggy-haired twenty-six-year-old who lived with his parents.

The police were going through the motions on their end. Carver reactivated Misty's name on state and national lists but only because he was legally required to do so. At this point, he still believed Misty to be a runaway and doubted Diana's veracity.

Meanwhile, Diana would find Cory Bober's constant badgering to be annoying. It got so bad she filed a restraining order against him.

"My daughter has been missing for six weeks from the Puyallup Fair," Diana wrote in the restraining order. "Cory Bober has called me on a daily basis, telling me my daughter is dead. I was advised by Deputy Brian Coburn to file this complaint if I felt threatened."

The order would only last two weeks. Diana would then call the courts and rescind her request. She would later call Bober and apologize. Her daughter had been missing for over 56 days. Bober was annoying as hell but he was the only one doing research. The only one who cared.

Bober organized a volunteer search for Misty in the Green River area. He somehow coerced someone on the police forensic team to tell him the general vicinity of where one of the Puyallup girl's body was found. Bober surmised that Misty's body would be found in the same general area.

Seventy-two days after Misty had gone missing, there was now a volunteer team searching for her.

Nothing came out of the search.

But Diana would later spot Rheuban at a grocery store and confront him. The young man ran and got into a truck with an older man. She saw the look of fear and apprehension on both men as they sped off.

Diana would then lapse into a depression. She tried to commit suicide with booze and prescription drugs.

The next day she would wake up in a hospital. She would spend the next day there, drying out until being discharged back into the nightmare that had become her life.

A PLEA TO THE PUBLIC

Four months after Misty's disappearance, Diana would appear on a local TV station for a special on the Green River Killer. Jim Doyon, the homicide detective who worked the case, spoke of the killings but deferred on stating if Delange and Chebetnoy(the slain Puyallup girls) were connected.

Doyon took an interest in Misty's case. He would journey to Highway 410 and search near milepost 30 where the bodies of Delange and Chebetnoy had been discovered.

Like Bober and the volunteer search team, he too came up empty.

Bober was undaunted and organized another search. He realized that they had been searching in the wrong spot. They were searching on the south side of the highway when the should have been searching on the north.

Twelve people would show up for the search. Diana would arrive with her older sister, Debra. Bober would arrive with Al Hensley, the father of one of the slain Puyallup girls along with his 14-year old Boy Scout nephew, Jaremy Brown.

It would be the Boy Scout that would make the find

Poking into a ditch with his stick, he saw the crumpled blue jeans. Socks fell out of the jeans.

Baggy and stone-washed, they were cuffed at the bottom. The same jeans that Misty had borrowed from her mother on the night of the fair. The jeans were too big for her and Diana remembered them cuffing them on the bottom.

Bober became excited. He knew that the killer had planted the jeans there as a taunt.

He was right. The police were wrong.

But Diana, according to her sister, "broke into a million pieces."

THE KILLING FIELD

Seven dead women had been found in the nine-mile stretch between Enumclaw and Greenwater in the eight years prior to Misty's disappearance.

The two slain Puyallup girls were found in the same area in 1988 and 1991, only one hundred feet apart. They were left off a footpath that had been hidden by thick brush.

Both of the teenage girls had been presumed abducted from the Puyallup shopping center. Detective Jim Doyon believed privately that the cases were connected. He arrived at the site where Misty's jeans were found and interviewed witnesses, particularly Diana and Bober.

The jeans were taken to the lab and the forensic analysis indicated that the jeans had been in the ditch for some time.

Police suspected that someone (Bober? Diana?) had planted the jeans there.

What was undeniable that the jeans were found only a ten minute walk away from where the bodies of the two slain Puyallup girls were found.

SUSPICIONS ARISE

People began to talk. There were reporters who believed the jeans were planted there. Some were talking as if Diana and Bober were lovers and had plotted this for some insurance money.

Dede Miles, a fifteen-year-old friend of Misty, would come to Sgt. Carver with a tip. She said there was a boy that kept coming over to Misty's parties. He would always leave before her mother came home.

His name was Rheuban Schmidt.

Finally, the unkempt looking young man would come under the radar of the police.

Diana, meanwhile, began to suspect Cory Bober.

How did he know where to look? Why was this stranger so interested in the case to begin with? How did he know so much?

The police had warned her to stay away from him. Now she felt compelled to tell the police of her suspicions.

"Diana comes to station. Now feels Cory Bober may be involved in Misty's disappearance. I asked Diana to submit a written statement to that effect and why she feels he may be involved – she agreed to do so."

Carver's notes

AN INTERVIEW WITH TRINA

Detective Jim Doyon would interview the fifteen-year-old Trina Bevard, the last person to see Misty alive.

Six months had passed. Doyon had brought along the jeans with him, the sight of which made Trina cry.

"It seems to me like something that Misty was wearing that night," Trina said. "It looks very close to what Misty was wearing. The socks, they match what she was wearing. The jeans are big, so – her jeans were baggy that night, that she was wearing. They're – they were light blue like they are in the photo. It just seems, you know, it was the clothes that she was wearing."

Doyon would go on to ask what she was wearing (a pullover) and if she had any jewelry. He then asked if she had any cigarettes or birth control pills.

"No," Trina said. "She was straight. She was a virgin. She didn't smoke, she didn't drink, she didn't do drugs. She was clean, so she had no reason to do anything. She wasn't sexually active."

Trina then revealed that the girls made five calls to Rheuban. They could not get a hold of him. They finally got him on the line and he still refused to pick them up even when the girls offered him money. Misty told him about a key under the front doormat of her home. He could go inside, get money for gas and come pick them up.

Trina stated that she didn't trust Rheuban but only because he didn't keep his word and come pick them up. She then called a 23-year old friend named Mike Rhyner for a ride but they got disconnected. The girls were then stranded. They walked downtown to get to the bus stop before spotting a phone booth by a convenience store. Misty then called her mother, telling her that if Rheuban didn't come pick her up she would take the bus. The two argued as Diana didn't want Misty around Rheuban.

Trina had to get home by 10 p.m. She had about an hour and a half to get home which wasn't that far. Misty could not walk the ten miles to Spanaway.

Trina then decided to walk. She gave Misty her extra money for the bus.

"At that time I made my decision of walking home and she said she would take the bus," Trina recalled. "The last words that I said to her were 'Be careful,' and she turned around and told me the same and we walked off in different directions"

Trina also dismissed the notion of Misty being a runaway.

" Her mom just bought her a stereo and she was so excited and she went shopping and she got new clothes,"Trina recalled. She was telling me all about it. She was really excited about it.

BOBER GOES TO JAIL

Meanwhile, Bober would be sentenced to fourteen months in prison for the marijuana possession. He felt that the sentencing was too punitive and threatened law enforcement that they would never find Misty without him. His fellow inmates thought he was crazy and began calling him "snitch" and "The Green River Killer".

Jail would not slow down Bober's efforts, however. He continued to research and write Misty's mother.

"Dear Diana,

...When we found Misty's clothes, part of me died and I watched a part of you die too (much more than a "part") and I was at a total loss for words. I never wanted to be the one to show you your most horrible fears were true and that your daughter is truly dead at the hands of a sick murderer. I will never rest until the killer (Randy Achziger) is brought to justice and dead, if it takes my life to do it."

AMERICA'S MOST WANTED

Misty's case would eventually be broadcast nationally as it was featured on the America's Most Wanted television show.

Over twenty-eight tips came into Sgt. Carver from people who watched the broadcast.

When the tips went nowhere, Diana's suspicions returned to her original suspect, Rheuban Schmidt. She wanted Carver to speak to the young man but the Sergeant would take a circuitous route to get to Schmidt.

Carver would speak to Frank Rodriguez, the owner of Adam's Ribs, a restaurant where Rheuban worked. He convinced the owner to try and find out how much Rheuban knew about Misty.

"3-4-93 @ 1500: Frank states Rheuban said the following during a lengthy conversation about Misty Copsey:

- Yeah, I know about it.

- I know exactly where she is buried.

- They found the clothes but she is buried 6 miles from there.

- They're off by 6 or 6 1/2 miles."

— Excerpt from Carver's notes

Carver would then wait for Rheuban outside the restaurant before his shift started. Schmidt arrived, saw the cops and immediately ran off. The detectives would eventually catch up with him.

Rheuban would concede that he had received calls from Misty the night of her disappearance. But his story corroborated with Trina's, he told the girls he had no gas and could not pick them up.

Carver then asked if he knew where Misty was buried but Rheuban was adamant that he "said those things to get Frank off my back."

Rheuban then revealed that he suffered from "black outs". He stated that he did not recall anything until the daylight hours of September 18th, 1992.

The detectives pounced, asking if it was possible that he blacked out, picked up Misty and harmed her.

Rheuban claimed he didn't know.

All he knew was that he drove out to his grandmother's farmhouse and couldn't recall why.

Detectives would then give Rheuban a polygraph test.

They would later state that the suspect "zoned out" during the test, nearly falling asleep. The tests were inconclusive but detectives felt as if he were trying to beat the test.

A LITTLE LIE

Rheuban fell off the detective's radar when Carver talked to Dede Miles again. Dede would tell the detective that Trina had not walked home from the fairground like she told him.

Dede said that Trina had a boyfriend come pick her up and didn't want anyone to know.

Trina's boyfriend's name was Michael J. Rhyner. He had nothing on his record aside from traffic stops but he had friends that were connected with Chebetnoy and Delange.

He also had a complaint when he was sixteen years old. He was accused of an abduction rape wherein he used a knife and a cigarette lighter to terrorize an eleven-year-old.

Charges were never filed for an undisclosed reason.

Carver brought Trina in for more questioning. He wanted the truth. The truth about who picked her up that night. The truth about Misty.

But the truth was that Trina told the Sgt. Carver and Detective Tom Matison that she lied because she feared "getting into trouble with her guardian about it."

Trina admitted that she called Rhyner, got disconnected and left a message. She told Misty that they could both ride with Rhyner but Misty said no.

"Trina would not be specific why Misty did not trust Rhyner, but the indication was that Rhyner might have 'come on' to Misty at one time and she did not like it. Trina states that she and Rhyner are friends, but not involved."

— Matison's notes

Trina said that she started to walk and then Rhyner picked her up and dropped her off. The detectives asked if perhaps Rhyner had picked up Misty but she said no.

FRANK RODRIGUEZ' FOLLOW UP

Diana would state that Frank Rodriguez, Rheuban's employer, would call her to say that Rheuban had "bragged about doing something" to Misty with his uncle. Frank didn't fully believe him, however, as Rheuban was "weird" and always bragging about stuff he didn't do.

Diana then approached Carver about Rheuban and the sergeant went ballistic.

"We have our man!" he said.

The man he sought was Michael Rhyner, Trina Bevard's boyfriend.

"We share our knowledge of Mike Rhyner and how he is involved with Misty and Trina – and the fact Trina lied to Doyon. We state that there is an excellent possibility that Rhyner may be linked to Chebetnoy and DeLange. Exchange of information is extremely beneficial."

— Carver's notes

"Sgt. Carver believes that Rhyner dropped Bevard off, returned to the area of the fairgrounds, located Misty Copsey, convinced her to get into his vehicle and drove off with her."

— Doyon's notes

Police set up a sting on Rhyner. The car mechanic was selling his 1981 blue Ford Escort for $200 bucks.

The buyer was an undercover cop.

He watched as Rhyner hurriedly took out trash from the car before the sale. The police then did a forensic examination of the car.

Meanwhile, Rheuban's green Nova was being crushed at a wrecking yard. The Puyallup police didn't care as the tweaker was no longer on their radar. Also, Randy Achziger, Bober's suspect, had been charged and convicted for the rape of a seven-year-old.

INTERROGATING RHYNER

Ideally, Detectives Matison and Sgt. Carver wanted the forensics back from Rhyner's Escort before they spoke to him. But the wait became interminable and they brought him in for questioning without some evidence to back up their suspicions.

Rhyner's story would match that of Trina's. He picked Trina up and went back home. He said that he and Trina were only "good friends" and he had met Misty only four times. Matison then asked Rhyner if he felt Misty was alive and what should happen to the person who harmed her.

Rhyner knew what the detective was getting at. On his own volition, Rhyner told the detectives about his juvenile complaint from years ago. He stated he had been cleared and knew that was why they were looking at him now.

"First thing I thought, you know, well, that's in my file," Rhyner said. "Now you guys are going to think I did it since it's in my file. About Misty, that's the one thing that worried me."

Rhyner then passed a polygraph test.

Grasping at straws, the police then turned their sights back on Rheuban. If only they had impounded his car when they had the chance...

TOO LITTLE TOO LATE

"Rheuban Schmidt's initial interview with Sgt. Carver and I created more questions than answers. He was very vague about what he did that September 17th and finally said that he had a 'blackout' and 'woke up' at his grandmother's property near Enumclaw.

...Schmidt had told Frank Rodriguez that Misty's body was six miles from where the jeans were found. He now claims that he said this just to get Rodriguez "off his back," and was not a true statement.

He was driving a Green Chev Nova at the time but he no longer has the vehicle. It was repossessed.

Schmidt also mentioned that his Grandmother's property is located in King County by Buckley and is over a hundred acres. The property has cows on it. Few people enter onto the property."

— Matison's notes

Tinsley, fifteen years old at the time of Misty's disappearance, told police the Rheuban was his roommate for only a few months. He described Rheuban as a short-tempered guy who had a thirteen-year-old girlfriend. The girlfriend, Tinsley said, got jealous when Rheuban got a call from Misty.

Tinsley stated that Rheuban had left the apartment in a huff then came back between eleven and one at night.

So Rheuban did not "black out" as he told detectives. N

"What do you think might have happened to her?" Matison asked.

"Um, I couldn't, I couldn't say because I have no idea," Tinsley said.

"Well, can you speculate?"

"With Rheuban, this is just that I, this, this is what I say with Rheuban because I, I figure that um that he, he tried to, he tried to um, get with her or something and she said, she said no and he got all pissed and did something, I don't know, that's just a second guess."

"You think Rheuban would be capable of ah, kidnapping and killing somebody?"

"I think he could," Tinsley said.

Detectives would meet with Rheuban again, relaying the information that Tinsley recalled him coming back to the apartment that night.

But Rheuban remained adamant in stating that he didn't remember what he did. The detectives then drove him out to his grandmother's farm which had over 100-acres...100 secluded acres.

Detective Matison would note that Rheuban's grandmother's house six miles north of Buckley. Rheuban told Frank that Misty would be buried six miles away from where her jeans were found which would place it in the close vicinity of his grandmother's farm. They would go to inquire with his grandmother but she was not home.

They did not follow-up with the grandmother .

Even so, Rheuban's story no longer held up. He told Misty that he didn't have any gas. He lived sixteen miles away from the fair.

But then he stated that he had driven to his grandmother's farm in Buckley then returned home.

A sixty-mile round trip.

Detectives would give him another polygraph test which he passed.

"It appears that Rheuban Schmidt was not involved in the disappearance of Misty Copsey. He, however, has no alibi as to his movements during the evening of her disappearance, as well as no memory; he claimed that he had a blackout. He acknowledges that he left the residence of James Tinsley, but does not remember what he did.

Investigation to continue."

— Matison's notes

ONE YEAR ANNIVERSARY

The local media ran a few more stories on Misty's disappearance as the Puyallup Fair started. The forensic test on Rhyner's test finally came through. There was no match

with Misty anywhere.

Now once again grasping at straws, Carver would turn to Diana and her associates. He would interview Diana's parole officer and one of her ex-boyfriends.

Misty's father, Buck, was asked to take a polygraph test. He gave consent and passed.

"I explained to her that missing person investigations, at some point in time, must eliminate the parents of any wrongdoing. Diana agreed to the examination."

— Carver's notes

Diana would pass her polygraph test but Jim Corey, Doyon's colleague, said that Diana's polygraph would prove to be inconclusive and that perhaps she had something to do with planting the jeans at the location on Hwy 410.

Carver had always had his doubts about Diana and felt that she planted the jeans.

But the leads would eventually dry up. After nine years, Misty Copsey's disappearance would turn cold.

No one was ever charged with her disappearance.

THE AFTERMATH

Diana would hand out fliers at the Puyallup Fairgrounds every year. She was doing more than law enforcement and even the media.

Every now and then, a local reporter would run a story about Misty. A few cranks would call in and say that they knew something but it would lead to nowhere. Then that would be it. Everything would run dry.

Detective Jim Doyon felt that she was deceased.

BOBER TO THE RESCUE

Bober was then caught for marijuana possession again but this time, he pressed for an advantage. He would gain the Washington State Patrol crime lab report on Misty's jeans, compiled after their 1993 discovery.

He argued that the lab report was part of his defense....he gambled and won.

Obtaining the prized document, the amateur sleuth went to work. The report stated there was no blood, no semen. But there were hairs, fibers, and three red paint chips. There were also holes in the left leg in the jeans, above the knee.

Bober knew that somehow, someway, Randy Achziger was involved. That he killed Misty.

The forensic details raced through Bober's head...red paint chips...red paint chips...

He knew that Bober had a red Porsche. He knew that the paint chips would match.

But the police had another suspect they didn't tell anyone about.

Robert Leslie Hickey.

Hickey's hunting ground was the Puyallup area where he specialized in abduction rapes.

He also drove a red Camaro.

Puyallup police had him on their list as a possible suspect but he was never questioned nor did they obtain forensic samples from his car.

Thirteen years later, however, they would collect samples from Achziger's old car. The car had been sold and the new owner was open to having forensics performed on it.

The particles would be sent to a crime lab which already had a backlog of over a year.

With nothing else left to do, the police turned once again to Rheuban Schmidt.

"I think it's worth taking another shot at Schmidt, and we're planning on it. He's been clean since 1993 ...

— Excerpt from notes by Lt. Dave McDonald, March 19, 2006

Only Schmidt had not been clean. He had been convicted of second-degree theft in 2000. In early 1996, he was accused of rape by one of Misty's best friends. He had held a pillow over her face to silence her but two weeks after filing the report, the girl back away from her accusation and did not file charges.

"[She] told me that she would be undergoing counseling related to the rape, but that she did not want to undergo any additional stress that may be caused by further investigation or possible prosecution in this matter.

Case cleared exceptional/refused by victim."

— Pierce County sheriff's report, Feb. 6, 1996

Later in 2006, Puyallup police gathered more reports on Rheuban. One was a domestic violence protection order requested by his wife, the mother of his three children.

"Rheuban has previously told her that if she ever had him served with a court order he'd 1) burn her house down with her and her kids in it, and 2) send 'some guys' to kick in her door and take money from her.

(She) said Rheuban told her that they'd get money from her if they had to beat her, rape her and then rob her.

(She) said Rheuban told her that if it came to that she 'wouldn't be breathing' when they were done with her."

— Pierce County Sheriff's report, Nov. 9, 2006

MISSING PAINT CHIPS

Adding more incompetence to the investigation, the red paint chips found on Misty's jeans would turn up "missing." All that remained inside the bag where the chips were marked was a piece of plastic.

The lab technicians now had no way to match the red chips on Misty's jeans to Achziger's red Porsche.

Bober would claim that the red chips did match and the police were now trying to save face. Diana, however, no longer wants anything to do with him.

Bober would state that the police would tell Diana that they had, in fact, tested the red paint found on Misty's clothes against Achziger's Porsche. Bober discovered that the red paint was missing beforehand yet the police would lie to Diana about the test.

The lies and incompetence that began investigation have seemingly ended it as well. The Puyallup police relied far too heavily on polygraph tests to discount suspects where their own accounts (particularly in the case of Schmidt) were shaky at best. They failed to secure possession of Schmidt's Green Nova which may have proven to provide forensic evidence that Misty was in his vehicle.

Twenty-four years have elapsed since Misty's disappearance.

Her case remains unsolved.

MISSING TIFFANY

ANA BENTON

The Disappearance of Tiffany Daniels

As shocking as it might seem, there are over 100,000 missing person cases active in the United States this very second. While the majority of them are eventually found, there is a large percentage of those who have been gone for years. The police extended their investigations as much as they could, and they reached the very end because there was no new information. Finally, those cases simply turn cold.

Missing person cases are particularly difficult for both families and friends. All of them are left without answers about what happened to their loved one, and they are constantly waiting for a break in the case, hoping they will have closure. The Daniels family lived through all of this in the summer of 2013 when their daughter Tiffany went missing one afternoon. It is one of the most perplexing cases in the history of Pensacola, Florida that still puzzles the investigators.

Early life

Tiffany Daniels was born on March 11th, 1988 in Dallas, Texas. She grew up in a loving and supportive family who encouraged her to follow her dreams from an early age. Tiffany loved arts, and that was evident since her high school days. She was very creative and would spend days working on a single painting. Tiffany was not shy at all and had many friends who loved spending time with her because she was always happy and positive.

After finishing high school, Tiffany felt the need to change her scenery so she moved out to Pensacola, Florida. The city had everything Tiffany craved for – long beaches, beautiful nature, and great artistic community. She was an avid hiker and loved spending time in nature. Not to forget that she often went camping on her own just to clear up her mind and relax. Tiffany loved animals, and she was a pescetarian, meaning that her diet didn't contain any meat except for the fish. She also accepted a position at Pensacola State College theater as a set designer. The pay was not spectacular, but Tiffany was doing what she loved, and she could release her artistic side.

Tiffany liked to express herself through dancing as well. It was the perfect way for her to wind down, and she would frequent blues and swing parties downtown. Everyone in those circles knew Tiffany and loved her house gatherings too. Once the dance party comes to an end, Tiffany's friends would get in their vehicles and continue having fun at her home. She was spontaneous, loved the people around her, and enjoyed life to the fullest.

Unfortunately, her caring nature got her into financial problems. Tiffany mostly lived with roommates because she was not able to cover the whole rent herself. However, those roommates would often miss their payments, and Tiffany felt bad for them. She would always pay their share even though she was struggling herself. Unfortunately, those roommates would use her kindness, and they never pay Tiffany back. In the end, Tiffany's bank account was almost empty, and she was looking for a responsible roommate who could actually afford to live with her. She ended up placing a Craigslist ad, hoping she would have more luck with the next roommate.

Gary Nichols who was 54 years old at the time saw the ad and contacted Tiffany since he needed a place to stay as soon as possible. Gary was the father of one of Tiffany's friends, and he was going through a divorce. Even though the difference in age was evident, Tiffany accepted her new roommate with open arms, and the two of them started getting along really well. Gary was financially stable, so Tiffany knew that the rent will not be a problem for him. Additionally, they had similar interests because Gary was very active, and both of them followed the same diet. Gary moved in during July of 2013, and Tiffany hoped that her issues with tenants were over.

Tiffany was in a relationship at the time, and her boyfriend's name was Grey Thomas. They met in the summer of 2012 at a dance party and were inseparable since then. He just got accepted to the graduate program at the University of Texas located in Austin. He decided to move there and urged Tiffany to join him. However, Tiffany was not eager to leave Florida, but she still wanted to have a long-distance relationship with him. The two have made plans for her to visit in a couple of weeks, and Tiffany was happy because it was clear he cared about her as well. Grey hoped Tiffany will like Austin and that she would eventually change her mind about moving there.

The day of the disappearance

Tiffany's boyfriend was supposed to head out to Texas on August 11th, 2013 and the two of them met for a breakfast where they said goodbyes to each other. They will be apart for a couple of weeks and simply had to spend some time together before his trip. Gary Nichols saw Tiffany that afternoon, and he did notice that she was a bit sad about the fact that her boyfriend was leaving which was understandable. But she soon started talking about the trip to Austin she was planning and her mood brightened up immediately.

Since Pensacola State College theater was preparing to start the production of the musical called *Spamalot*, Tiffany had a lot of work ahead of her. *Spamalot* was based on the movie called *Monty Python and the Holy Grail* so Tiffany decided to re-watch it just to get inspired. After all, she was in charge of the set and wanted to do a great job. Gary Nichols was at the house, so he joined her in front of the TV set. The two watched the movie up until midnight and then went to sleep. Both of them had to get up early for work. Sometime around 05:00 AM Gary heard the front door opening and closing several times. He thought it must be Tiffany, but he was a bit confused because he knew that she was not an early riser. As a matter of fact, her job started at 08:00 AM so this was very unusual.

Gary got up and went work at 07:00 AM. The first thing he noticed when he exited the house was that Tiffany's car was gone. He assumed she went to work earlier because it was the first day of *Spamalot* production. Tiffany probably wanted to get more things done. Tiffany's boss did confirm that she showed up for work on schedule but asked him to leave earlier. Tiffany also mentioned that she will not be in town for a couple of days and wanted to inform him about it. Tiffany didn't mention where she was going and didn't provide any additional information. The boss simply concluded that she might have some family business, or wanted to go camping. Tiffany left the theater around 04:45 PM.

Gary came home from work as usual but Tiffany wasn't there. It was strange because she didn't mention she was leaving or anything similar. Tiffany was very responsible and would always tell her friends and family about her plans. Even though Gary was her roommate for a short time, he got to know Tiffany and was sure that she would bring up an upcoming trip. Gary called his daughter Noel who was Tiffany's friend and asked her if she knew anything about Tiffany's whereabouts. She told him not to worry and that Tiffany would show up soon because she was probably staying with friends or working overtime.

The power was cut off the next day, and Gary assumed that Tiffany forgot to pay the bills. He tried contacting her, but nobody answered the cell phone. Worried that something happened to her, he once again urged his daughter Noel to contact Tiffany's mother Cindy and see if she could get a hold of her. Noel sent her a Facebook message, and Tiffany's mother brushed it off because her daughter was a free spirit and had a tendency to go out in nature. Perhaps she had no signal, or she didn't hear the phone ringing. But as the days went on without a single word from Tiffany, everyone started feeling a bit uneasy about the situation.

The search for Tiffany

Tiffany's family got really concerned after they realized that they couldn't reach her for several days. Her cell phone kept ringing, but nobody was answering. Cindy Daniels decided to start calling Tiffany's friends to see if anyone knew where her daughter was. She contacted Noel Nichols, and the two of them made a list of people they should contact. As they went through the list, they realized that no one had seen Tiffany for a week and they all assumed she was staying with another friend. Cindy was really worried, and she contacted the law enforcement to report that her daughter was missing.

Cindy went straight to Escambia County sheriff's office, but the law enforcement didn't take her seriously. They did send out a patrol car to her house to take a statement. The officers thought that since Tiffany was young and free-spirited, she is probably somewhere having a blast and she would turn up soon. But Cindy persisted, and they took a closer look at the case. Escambia County sheriff's office realized that the missing person case was not in their jurisdiction because Tiffany lived in Pensacola and that was also the location she was last seen at. Pensacola Police Department was not dismissive of the report, and they were quickly out on the scene.

Cindy was already at Tiffany's place of residence when the detective Daniel Harnett arrived there to investigate if there was anything suspicious in the house. Tiffany's mother was asked to wait in front of the house. The detective and an officer went through the rooms together and found Tiffany's camping gear. This meant that she wasn't taking a break somewhere in the woods. There were also no signs that she packed her things for any type of trip. Detective Harnett asked Cindy about Tiffany's personal life, focusing on her boyfriend Grey Thomas. Cindy told him that he left for Texas one day before Tiffany's disappearance and this made Detective Harnett focus on the possibility that Tiffany decided to follow him there. However, one of Tiffany's closest friends said: *"Tiffany was a very spontaneous person, but she was also a reliable person. My opinion is if she said that she would be somewhere, she would be there."*

Rodney Daniels, Tiffany's father called Grey Thomas to see if she was there with him. He told him that he spoke to Tiffany on the day of his arrival to Texas, but he hasn't heard from her afterward. Knowing that the majority of disappearances are often followed by a murder, Detective Harnett couldn't rule out the option that Grey returned to Pensacola one day later and hurt Tiffany for some reason. He contacted Grey, asking him to go to his local police station and give them his DNA. They needed to have it in a database in case some new evidence turns up during the investigation. Curious about Grey's whereabouts on the day of the disappearance, Detective Harnett requested Grey's cellphone data. It showed that Grey was in Austin, Texas since the day he left Pensacola.

Running out of reasons for the disappearance, the investigators started interviewing the entire family. They started viewing the case as a possible suicide, so Detective Harnett asked a lot of questions about Tiffany's mental state. Her sister Candace McAdams who lived out of state was very close to Tiffany. The two of them spoke over the phone at least a couple of times every week. Candace mentioned that she noticed a change in Tiffany's behavior sometime in 2012. She was not as happy as she used to be and Candace though that she might be keeping something from her. But nobody could be certain that she was depressed or had any mental problems.

After questioning the neighbors, the investigators found out that Tiffany did come back home after work on the day of her disappearance. Her car was seen briefly in front of the house. Gary Nichols was there at the time, but he didn't see her come in. He was talking with his girlfriend on the phone, and the chances are he was simply too engaged in the conversation to register that someone opened the front door. Cindy thought this was strange because the house itself wasn't large. She stated: *"In Tiffany's room the top of her closet had a foot missing of it. Clear through to the next room. You could throw something through it. I find it hard to believe he couldn't hear her through the room but he heard her going in and out of the house early in the morning."* However, the police dismissed Gary as a suspect because there were no traces of foul play anywhere, and he was the first one to start worrying about Tiffany. Detective Hartnett said: *"Gary seemed appropriate. There was nothing unclear in anything he told us to raise an alarm."*

The discovery of the car

Detective Harnett alerted the media right away about Tiffany's 1999 Toyota 4Runner car, hoping that someone might have seen it somewhere. The TV stations broadcasted the images for days, while Tiffany's friends went around Pensacola, putting up the fliers. And soon enough, the police had their first solid lead. Tiffany's car was spotted at a parking lot at Park West in Pensacola Beach. A jogger who was out running on the morning of August 20th, 2013 thought that the vehicle looked familiar and connected the dots. He also knew the Daniels family, as well as Tiffany herself. Tiffany's mother said: *"I felt something bad happened as soon as they located the car. I believed she was still on the island and that we would find her."*

Once the police arrived, they inspected the abandoned car. It was not too dirty from the outside, and it looked like it was out in the elements for a couple of days. They found Tiffany's bicycle on the inside, alongside her purse, a wallet, a cell phone, a couple of paintings, a jar of peanut butter, and a bottle of water. The forensic team analyzed the car and found two suspicious fingerprints on the car and the steering wheel. After a thorough examination, they determined that the fingerprints didn't belong to Tiffany or any of the officers who were on the scene. Then they proceeded to run them through the database but got no hits.

The parking lot where the car was found was right next to the beach. It was a very popular spot for both locals and tourists. Tiffany's friends and family though that someone must have seen something in the days following the disappearance. The police weren't enthusiastic about it because Tiffany's car was not very distinctive and they were certain nobody would have noticed when it arrived or who was driving it. Not to forget that there were two condominium complexes on the other side of the parking lot. It was summertime and people would usually hang out on their balconies, trying to cool down from the heat.

Tiffany's friends started going around, handing out the flyers, and talking to the people living in the apartment buildings. One resident told them that he was sure the car was not in the parking lot two days ago because he has a good view of it and would have noted if a particular vehicle was parked there for a longer period of time. A couple of people said that they saw a man driving and exiting the car. All of the information was written down and presented to the detectives. They were conducting their own investigation at the time that included toll booths at the Bob Sikes Bridge.

Since Park West was located on Santa Rosa Island, only one bridge connected it to the mainland. The bridge has toll booths, and every vehicle that crosses over is captured by the surveillance cameras. Unfortunately, the cameras monitor the license plates only so finding out who was driving the car was impossible. On the other hand, this information would provide the investigators with the exact time when Tiffany's Toyota crossed the bridge. The detectives went through the images of vehicles that entered Santa Rosa Island on the day Tiffany disappeared and discovered that her car passed the toll booths on August 12th, 2013 at 07:51 PM. This was three hours after she left the theater.

The search of Santa Rosa Island

The detectives, as well as the family, had many theories about what might have happened to Tiffany on Santa Rosa Island. The forensic team determined that the tires of her bike had sand on them which led them to speculate that she went on a ride that night. She might have placed the bike in her car and proceeded to the beach to watch the meteor shower or take a swim in the ocean. The currents are incredibly strong in that area, and she could have been pulled under, unable to swim back to the shore.

Led by this thought, the detectives suspected that her body might appear on the shore of Santa Rosa Island. The island itself was large and searching it would be quite a task. Tiffany's parents found out about KLAAS organization that would gather up the volunteers from the area in order to search for missing children. They contacted the people in charge, and they agreed to help out with the search of Santa Rosa Island. The teams had a lot of grounds to cover, but they had plenty of help from the other search organizations in Florida. They searched the island by foot, going through the entire national park. There was no sign of Tiffany or any items that could be connected to her.

The fact that they didn't find any traces was encouraging to Tiffany's family because this meant that she might be alive somewhere. But it was unlikely that she was still on the island. They needed to widen up the search and let everyone know that Tiffany was missing. Noel Nichols decided to set up a Facebook page in order to help find Tiffany. She uploaded her photos as well as the images of her distinctive foot tattoos. Other users were sharing the information, and soon the tips started coming in.

The sightings

Noel sent every single information she got through the Facebook page to the detective working on this case. Detective Daniel Harnett, eager to find Tiffany, was willing to check every possible sighting. A few weeks after setting up the page, Noel received a tip from a local store. A clerk claimed that Tiffany entered the shop and bought some groceries. He was able to provide a full description of the girl which sparked the interest. Unfortunately, Detective Harnett asked for the surveillance tapes, and Tiffany was not on them. The clerk simply wanted to become a part of the investigation at any cost.

But the next possible sighting gave Tiffany's parents hope that she was out there somewhere. A waitress from Metairie, Louisiana sent a message through Facebook in January of 2014 saying that she might have seen Tiffany a couple of weeks after her disappearance. The woman didn't contact anyone because she was not sure if the girl in the restaurant was indeed Tiffany. However, she couldn't stop thinking about it and decided to let the family know. There was something strange about that encounter, and the waitress thought that it might be important.

She recalls that three women came into the restaurant one night. Two of them were younger, while the third one was significantly older than them. The older woman wore expensive clothes, while the other two did not. They also had long sleeved shirts, which was an odd sight in New Orleans during the summer and autumn. The waitress found it unusual that the older woman was the only one communicating with her. The young women simply sat there in silence, trying not to make an eye contact with the waitress. One of them spoke up to ask if the soups on the menu had fish in them, and the waitress took a good look at her face. It seemed familiar to her and she asked right away if she was the woman who went missing in Florida.

The mood at the table shifted instantly. The whole group got up and left the restaurant. The tip sounded credible because Tiffany was a pescetarian, and she was very concerned about her diet. The family asked if the waitress could provide any surveillance videos that would give them proof that Tiffany was there. She told them that the tapes were long gone because they record over the old footage regularly. While this didn't give the investigators any concrete proof that Tiffany was out there, the tip led Tiffany's family to form another theory – that she was a victim of human trafficking.

White Tiffany didn't fit the profile of a typical human trafficking victim, nothing can be dismissed in this case. There was a possibility that she was kidnapped from the beach and transported to New Orleans soon after her disappearance. Tiffany's family dug deeper and found connections with another incident when a young woman was taken to the same city by two men. She was then forced to become a sex worker. Human trafficking is an ongoing problem in the United States, and the police are doing everything in order to prevent it.

However, they simply cannot save all of the victims right away. Instead, they are familiar with the known human trafficking routes and the local patrol cars often monitor the movement on them. One of the routes is the Interstate 10 that passes through Pensacola. This very fact made Tiffany's parents believe that she met someone on the night of the disappearance and they probably took advantage of her. Tiffany was friendly and loved talking to other people. She might have bumped into someone who seemed trusting but had bad intentions. Unfortunately, the police still had little information, and they were unable to pursue this tip. The case remained open, but there were no new leads.

The revival of the case

The Investigation Discovery channel was aware of the case, and they decided to include it in the new season of their popular show called *Disappeared*. In it, they cover the missing person cases hoping that the media exposure would prompt the possible witnesses to contact the authorities and provide them with new details that could revive the case. Their crew visited Pensacola and talked to almost everyone involved with the investigation, including the lead detective and

Tiffany's parents. The whole city knew that the Investigation Discovery crew was there and people were once again talking about the case.

Four months after they completed the filming, Pensacola Police Department was contacted by a new eyewitness who claimed they had information about the case. The witness told Detective Hartnett that they saw a man opening the trunk of Tiffany's car on the parking lot in Park West. The man was wearing red shorts, and he was in his thirties. This confirmed the statements made by the tenants from the nearby apartment building who claimed that the vehicle was driven by a man. Unfortunately, they weren't able to identify the said individual.

Tiffany Daniels' disappearance is still being investigated, and the authorities are hoping that someone will come forward soon. There has not been a confirmed sighting since August 12th, 2013 but they are not ruling out the possibility that she is alive. The investigators never found her body, so any scenario is possible. The family and friends are managing the Facebook page about Tiffany, and they are updating it regularly, doing their best to keep her in the media. The case remains a true mystery that will hopefully be resolved one day.

THE DISAPPEARANCE OF KELSIE SCHELLING

ANA BENSON

Every time a woman goes missing or is found murdered, the police usually takes a closer look at their spouses or boyfriends. It is a standard procedure, especially if there were indications that they were in a troubled relationship. The disappearance of Kelsie Schelling is one of the biggest mysteries in Colorado. This young pregnant woman was last seen in February of 2013 and the case is still open to this day.

However, Kelsie's family was quite disappointed at the lack of interest by the police to investigate her then-boyfriend Donthe Lucas, who was clearly involved in this crime. After all, Donthe did invite Kelsie to his hometown on that fateful night and he was the last person who saw her alive. When they realized that the police are stalling with the investigation, the family made a promise that Kelsie's case will not be forgotten until they discover what really happened. They kept the public informed through their Facebook page and eventually managed to reach the Colorado Bureau of Investigation.

Early life

Kelsie Jean Schelling was born on 18th February 1991 in Holyoke, Colorado. She grew up in a tightknit family and later became even closer to her mother after the divorce of her parents. Kelsie was only eleven years old when they split up but she would often talk to her father as well. However, they didn't see each other that often because he moved to a different part of town. After graduating from high school, Kelsie attended Northeastern Junior College located in Sterling, Colorado. She was fascinated with psychology and planned to major in it once she gets accepted to the university.

Kelsie was friendly and outspoken, so it comes as no surprise that she had many friends and was a life of every party. During her time at Northeastern Junior College, Kelsie met Donthe Lucas. He was a star player on the basketball team and the two of them fell in love instantly. Donthe Lucas had a very difficult childhood and he grew up in Pueblo, Colorado which is an infamous place known for higher crime rates than anywhere else in the state. He loved basketball and it was clear that he would be an outstanding athlete even in high school. Basketball players do have enormous salaries so Donthe Lucas did see it as an opportunity to help his family out further down the line.

He was hoping that a scout would attend one of his games and recruit him for one of bigger colleges or universities that had a good basketball team. But his big break never happened. Instead, he ended up in Northeastern Junior College which was alright, but Donthe wasn't quite happy with that outcome. His dissatisfaction was evident even in the relationship with Kelsie. Their romance had constant ups and downs, and the two of them would break up, and get back together which drove Kelsie mad. They did finally call it quits after several semesters, and didn't see each other for quite some time.

After finishing the two years at the junior college, Kelsie pursued her education even further, and she moved to California to attend Vanguard University in Costa Mesa. She was finally able to study psychology full time. Donthe continued to play basketball for Emporia State University in Kansas. Kelsie's family was happy she managed to end her relationship with the troubled basketball player, and they hoped that she would make a new life far away from Colorado. Kelsie was independent and she enjoyed living and studying in California. When she wasn't attending classes, Kelsie worked at a tanning salon with her best friend. However, she did drop out of the college because the school work was a bit too much for her at the time and her only option was to go back home. She moved to Denver in 2012 and started working in a store. Meanwhile, Donthe Lucas was back in his hometown Pueblo.

The two of them started talking once again during the autumn of 2012. It was obvious that they still had feelings for each other, so no one was surprised when Donthe and Kelsie decided to spend the Christmas holidays together. The couple seemed happy to everyone around them, but Kelsie did tell her friends that their relationship was still very toxic. Donthe was still treating her badly, calling her names, and starting unnecessary fights. Soon enough everything will change. A few weeks after the holidays, Kelsie found out that she was pregnant. Shocked at first, Kelsie was lost and decided not to tell anyone for a couple of weeks. But keeping a secret was hard. So she called her mother and told her the news. Kelsie's mother Laura would later say that even though her daughter felt a bit stressed, she was still excited about the pregnancy. Yes, she was young but Kelsie was determined to make it work.

Donthe Lucas didn't take the news so well. Having in mind how dissatisfied he felt about his failed basketball career, it is not wrong to assume that the news about a baby simply solidified the fact that his dreams will never come true. Kelsie noticed the change in his mood and openly told him that he doesn't have to be a part of their baby's life. But it is also worth mentioning that Kelsie confided in her best friend that Donthe was ecstatic to become a father at one point. However, his mind was constantly changing. Kelsie went to see her doctor on 4th of February 2013 and he confirmed that she was eight weeks pregnant. The baby was healthy and doing well. The doctor provided her with an ultrasound of the unborn baby, and she was full of joy. Kelsie immediately sent out the pictures to her mother, her friends, and Donthe. Unfortunately, the excitement will not last forever.

The night of the disappearance

Donthe and Kelsey exchanged several emails on February 3rd, 2013. He invited her to visit him in Pueblo. She turned him down saying that she needs to go for a checkup the next day to make sure everything is alright with the baby. After seeing her doctor on the morning of February 4th, 2013, Kelsie went straight to the store. She worked the second shift and was expected to come home sometime after 10:00 PM that night. However, she was in contact with Donthe for the entire day, texting back and forth about the pregnancy. Donthe told her that she should drive out to Pueblo after work because he had a surprise for her. Not knowing what it is, Kelsie asked for more information because Pueblo is two hours away from Denver, and she would probably be tired after work. He insisted that she would be happy with his surprise and that he cannot tell her anything over the phone.

It is safe to assume that Kelsie thought that Donthe was ready to change and start a family with her. Their relationship wasn't a standard one but it seemed like Kelsie was willing to move past all the negative things and focus on the future. So after her shift ended, Kelsie got in her Chevy Cruze LTZ and drove to Pueblo in the middle of the night. Donthe was supposed to meet her in a parking lot in front of a local Walmart. The surveillance cameras did confirm that Kelsie got there on time, but Donthe was nowhere to be seen. She waited in a parked car for almost an hour before sending another text message to Donthe, saying that she has been in the parking lot for too long and that she would come pick him up at whatever location he is at the moment. She got a reply sometime around 12:15 AM.

Donthe told her that he will be waiting for her in the street next to his grandmother's home. Kelsie is seen exiting the parking lot a couple of minutes after she got the message. She clearly did arrive at the second rendezvous spot, but once again Donthe wasn't there. Kelsie sent him another message asking where is he and Donthe replied that he will be there in a minute. This is the last known communication between these two until sometime before 04:00 AM. After going through the phone records, police did discover that Donthe called Kelsie at 03:54 AM but she didn't pick up. The significance of this mysterious phone call will be revealed later. After reviewing the cell tower pings for both phones, the investigators did discover that they were in close proximity to each other.

The search for Kelsie

Kelsie's mother Laura got really worried the next day because she wasn't able to reach her daughter over the phone. She tried calling numerous times but it went straight to the voicemail. The last message she got from her daughter was the ultrasound image of her unborn child, and Laura wasn't sure if something happened to Kelsie after work, or she was ignoring her calls. Laura contacted Kelsie's friends who told her that she went to Pueblo to meet with Donthe. With no word from her daughter, she called Donthe who picked up his phone and told Laura that he had seen Kelsie last night, but that she drove back home in the morning.

Laura was starting to panic, but she did tell Donthe that she would involve the police if she doesn't hear from her daughter soon. Laura and Kelsie were very close and they did tell each other everything, but she suspected that her daughter kept this information from her because she didn't want Laura to know that she was meeting with Donthe. After all, Laura was aware of the nature of their relationship, and his reluctance to accept the baby. Plus, Laura would probably advise Kelsie not to go to Pueblo in the middle of the night.

Laura contacted the local law enforcement and told them that her daughter was missing. Without any solid leads or evidence, they started asking around for Kelsie. Their first step was to take a closer look at Donthe because he claimed that he was the last person to saw Kelsie. She did travel from Denver just to see him. After checking Kelsie's credit card records, they did notice that the card was used hours after Kelsie's last known contact with Donthe. They reviewed the surveillance of the ATM and noticed that Donthe had the card and picked up $400 from Kelsie's account. They weren't sure if Donthe had Kelsie's agreement to use the card, but that was a felony in the state of Colorado, so he was led to the police station for questioning. He had a lot of things to clear up, starting with the timeline of Kelsie's visit to Pueblo.

Donthe's interview

After being picked up by the police, Donthe told his own version of the story. They did see each other that night and talked until early morning hours. Donthe and Kelsie got into a fight and she felt too agitated to drive back home to Denver. She was also very tired from working the second shift. Instead, Kelsie decided to sleep in her car which was parked near his grandmother's house. According to Donthe, his phone rang sometime around 07:00 AM and it was Kelsie. She wasn't feeling well and asked Donthe to drive her to a hospital. He put on his clothes, got to her car, and drove her to the Parkview Hospital.

Kelsie wasn't sure if something happened to the baby during their argument last night and she insisted to see a doctor before she heads out to Denver. Donthe sat inside her car in the parking lot for two hours when she finally emerged from the hospital. Kelsie told him that she had lost the baby. She then asked Donthe to drive her to Walmart to get something to eat and buy some snacks for the road. The two of them started fighting while they were in Walmart and Kelsie refused to drive him home. Donthe simply walked away and got to his grandmother's house on foot. He didn't see Kelsie later in the day and he assumed she went home. He didn't mention stopping at the ATM to pick up the money during his initial interview.

The investigators did notice a couple of possible leads that could collaborate Donthe's story, namely the Parkview Hospital. Each medical facility keeps detailed records of the patients they treat. After speaking to the staff and going through the data, they have confirmed that Kelsie didn't check in during the morning of February 5th. There were also numerous surveillance cameras all over the building and none of them picked up Kelsie entering or leaving the hospital. It was obvious that this part of Donthe's story was not true.

Of course, the police investigators decided to check out Walmart as well because the parking lot and stores do have surveillance cameras, and they might have picked up something that would be of use. While they couldn't find Kelsie or Donthe entering the Walmart, they did notice Kelsie's car on the parking lot. However, the timeline didn't match up with Donthe's story because Kelsie's car appeared at noon, and not in the morning. Plus, Donthe was the only passenger in the car.

Another surveillance camera which was positioned on the back side of Walmart did record Donthe getting into his mother's car – another detail he failed to mention in the initial talk with the investigators.

Without any proof that Donthe's version of the events is true, they called him up for a second interview. The investigators did have a plan this time - they wanted to find out more about the ATM, and how it fits into his timeline. He told the detectives that he took $400 in order to pay his bills and that Kelsie lent him the money since he was at the ATM while Kelsie was at the hospital. When the detectives told Donthe that there is no record of Kelsie ever being in that hospital, his reply was: "I don't even know what to say right now."

They also presented him with Walmart surveillance video that proves Donthe was the only person in the car. He was surprised with the evidence put in front of him, and before the detectives managed to get him to open up, he decided to lawyer up. He was only charged with the identity theft due to the fact that he used Kelsie's credit card, but the case was dropped. The judge had determined that Donthe did use Kelsie's credit card in the past and it was a normal behavior. However, nobody managed to figure out why Donthe had her card in the first place. After all, if Kelsie decided to ran away and start a new life, she would need the money, as well as her vehicle.

Speaking of Kelsie's car, the investigators took a closer look at the surveillance video from Walmart parking lot because they wanted to follow the vehicle. Exactly one day after Donthe left Kelsie's car there, another man approached the car and got inside by using the key. He didn't break in or steal the car. The man was dressed in black, wearing a hoodie, so identifying him was almost impossible. His body type was different than Donthe's, and the mystery man was significantly shorter. Keep in mind that Donthe was a tall basketball player, so his height would be noticeable, even in a low-quality video.

Seeing the direction in which the car went, the police collected the surveillance videos from stores and businesses which were in close proximity. They put the puzzle pieces together and found a route but they couldn't follow it all the way. One day later, the car was dropped at the parking lot of Saint Mary Corwin Hospital. The man locked the car and walked away. The investigators located the vehicle on 14th of February, 2013 and figured out the timeline. But nobody knows where the car was during 6th of February. There weren't any signs of a struggle that would indicate that Kelsie was killed in her car. Almost all of her personal items were missing, including her wallet and a backpack.

While it is unclear if the vehicle was tested for the traces of DNA, an unnamed police officer who worked for Pueblo Police Department will later say that they did find bodily fluids in the trunk of Kelsie's car, as well as two palm prints. However, no one knows what happened with this evidence and was it ever tested. It is simply another thing which the police investigators decided to ignore in this case. Unfortunately, the whole investigation will be under scrutiny soon after.

Theories

Figuring out a solid theory without too many evidence or information can be challenging. Laura, Kelsie's mother, claims that her daughter was probably murdered and that it was premeditated. The first red flag for her was Donthe's initial invitation to meet him before the doctor's appointment. When Kelsie refused, he knew that he had to act fast. Donthe lured Kelsie to Pueblo by saying that he has something to show her, but he never gave an explanation to the law enforcement about what the surprise really was.

It is clear that Kelsie was alive and well up until the point she met Donthe in the street next to his grandmother's house. This is where the trail goes cold. The activity on her phone stops until 04:00 AM. If we analyze the location of the phones, another theory is that Donthe led Kelsie to a remote location and harmed her. It was possible that Kelsie dropped her phone in the middle of a struggle. Donthe couldn't find the phone in the dark, so he had to call her number. He was very likely getting rid of the evidence.

There is a possibility that the two of them did indeed get into a fight, and that an unfortunate accident happened. However, it is more likely that Donthe planned to get rid of Kelsie, and had planned every single step he would take that night. He really insisted to see her as soon as possible. While it is not fair to put the blame on the rest of Lucas family, the fact that his mother picked him up immediately after he left Kelsie's vehicle at the Walmart's parking lot indicates that she knew what was going on. Pueblo Police Department did stop investigating Donthe, and they claimed they didn't have enough physical evidence to prove that a crime really occurred. But they did receive a couple of noteworthy tips which were ignored and never pursued.

The missed opportunities

The entire investigation of the disappearance of Kelsie Schelling was troubling from the very beginning. While the detectives did not have physical evidence of a crime, it was clear that Donthe was the last person who saw Kelsie alive. In every standard investigation, he would have been the prime suspect, and the investigators would do their best to find more proof that he was somehow connected to the crime. The cell tower pings did show that both of their phones were in a remote area next to Pueblo in the early morning hours.

But there are even bigger missed opportunities that could have provided the investigators with the proof they needed. For instance, Donthe was living in his grandmother's house at the time of Kelsie's disappearance. However, the entire family moved out soon after. The landlord started redecorating the house because he wanted to rent it again. He did hear about the missing girl from Denver but had no idea about the details of the case, or the fact that the Lucas family was involved in any way.

He decided to put the new carpets in and when he lifted the old one, the landlord noticed a strange stain on the bottom. He contacted the police enforcement because he was worried that something bad has happened in the house. However, the police ignored his request to check out the stained carpet, and no one had ever arrived at Lucas' previous residence to pick it up. The landlord ended up throwing the carpet away because he simply couldn't keep it forever in the house and wanted to move on with the renovation.

Another missed opportunity involved a couple of fishermen who were out on a lake on a night fishing expedition. It is important to mention that the lake was located near the Saint Mary Corwin Hospital. As you might recall, that was the spot where the police officers discovered Kelsie's vehicle on the 14th of February 2013. They were out on a bank when a hook got stuck to something poking out of the sand. The fishermen went to investigate and were sure that they saw a part of a human ribcage, as well as a skull.

They were terrified by that discovery and left the area right away. Both of them were reluctant to notify the police because they did have some troubles with the law in the past. But that didn't stop them from telling this story to their friends who urged them to contact the local law enforcement. A couple of months passed before they finally talked to the police, but the lake wasn't searched afterward.

The current searches

Family and friends continued to search for Kelsie even after it was clear that the police enforcement forgot about her case. They created a Facebook group that was constantly updated with new information. Pueblo Police Department did go through many changes after Kelsie went missing. The lead investigator was replaced with a new one who was willing to cooperate with the Schelling family. The Schellings did offer a large reward for any new leads that might help them locate their missing daughter. The reward was $100,000 at one point.

This eventually led to false claims and misleading messages such as the one which claimed that Kelsie was still alive, but was placed into a sex traffic ring after a hired hitman decided not to kill her.

Laura Schelling contacted the police and told them about the message. Since the investigators decided to follow every lead possible, they dug deeper and even involved the FBI. Their experts did manage to trace the message back to Russia through the IP address so it was clear that this tip was useless.

The biggest break in the case happened in the spring of 2017 when Colorado Bureau of Investigation finally got the authorization from the local law enforcement to join the search. CBI did determine that the prime suspect should be Donthe Lucas, and they got the warrant to search the area around his previous place of residence. A large number of police officers was seen around that house during April of 2017, and they dug up the parts of the backyard using heavy machinery.

The search has been successful and the officers left the scene carrying bags of evidence. However, they stated that they didn't find any traces of Kelsie's remains. Kelsie's family released the following statement after the search: "The past 2 days have been grueling and emotional, ending with the outcome we did not hope for. Kelsie is still missing. There is no way for me to convey to you all the pain that I feel right now. Sincere, heartfelt thanks goes out to the members of Pueblo PD, CBI and Parks & Rec who worked so hard on this search for Kelsie. This was a physically demanding excavation for them and we witnessed how hard they worked. Despite all the issues we have had in the past, the new leadership over Kelsie's case from PPD and active involvement from CBI is giving us hope that an effective investigation is finally taking place."

The case is still active and the police didn't arrest Donthe. But the positive changes are happening and Kelsie's family is certain that they will find the answers they are looking for now that the investigation is finally moving forward.

FOREVER MISSING: THE DISAPPEARANCE OF NATALEE HOLLOWAY

NATHAN NIXON

Natalee Holloway Disappearance

The tragic story of Natalee Holloway still remains a mystery to this day. The events prior to her disappearance are centered on unreliable witnesses, investigators not following proper procedures, and friends who had left her alone with local patrons. To say that a school trip is never supposed to turn out this way is a monumental understatement. Several theories exist as to what really happened to Natalee. The one, glaring truth of the matter is that Natalee was a beautiful, vibrant young woman who is gone far too soon. Many other facts exist. Witnesses, however, do not.

Natalee Holloway was born in 1986 to David and Elizabeth Holloway in Clinton, Mississippi. Following her parents mutual divorce in 1993, she was raised by her mother alongside her younger brother. Natalee made her life in Alabama when her mother re-married to George Twitty. It was here that she prospered in many organizations, extracurricular activities, and academic niches. Natalee attended Mountain Brook High School in Mountain Brook, Alabama. She was a prominent member in the National Honor Society, was a leader on the school dance team, and competed several sports. Through her hard work, she had earned a full scholarship to attend the University of Alabama, where she enter a pre-med course track and eventually earn her Doctorate. This was all assuming she would make it to the next fall.

Upon graduation, 124 graduating Mountain Brook High School seniors took an "unofficial" school trip to Aruba. Aruba is a Dutch holding in the Caribbean. The group of students arrived in Aruba on May 26, 2005. The trip was scheduled for five days. Oddities of this trip were already apparent. While the trip had 7 chaperones, the students were not expected to be watched every second. The chaperones would meet with the full group of students each night to make sure that everything was okay. To say that these students were taking advantage of this was an understatement. "There was wild partying, lots of drinking, lots of room switching every night," Police Commissioner Gerold Dompig, who headed the investigation from mid-2005 to late 2016, said. "We are aware that the Holiday Inn told them they were absolutely not welcome back next year. Natalee, we know, drank all day every day while there. We have statements that proclaim she started every morning with cocktails. Often times so much drinking that she didn't show up for breakfast on two separate mornings."

Liz Cain and Claire Foreman, two of Holloway's classmates, agreed. "The drinking was excessive. We all were going too far and didn't understand the dangers"

Jodi Bearman organized the class trip. The investigation that would soon follow turned up numerous mistakes and irresponsibility's on the part of organizers and chaperones. The obvious problem was the supervision. How can seven chaperones have control of 124 high school graduates in a foreign place? These students were essentially given the freedom to do whatever they wanted with no punishment. Investigators and parents alike could not believe the lack of supervision and authority displayed by the adults. The punishment that Natalee Holloway would suffer was far greater than anyone could have imagined. However, the fact that this was an avoidable mistake is obvious. Natalee Holloway should never have been allowed to be in this position.

It was May 29, 2005. Natalee had packed her luggage and prepared all of her things to board the flight home the next morning. She had positioned her luggage neatly at the foot of her bed and cleaned up her hotel room accordingly. The 124 graduates had one last night of fun before it was time to head home. This was the last time she would be in her hotel room.

Natalee went out on the town with several of her classmates on night of May 29. Typical of the previous nights, she and her classmates had been heavily drinking and interacting with numerous locals. Natalee had a contagious personality and could always strike up a conversation with anyone. As the night drew on into morning, they arrived at Carlos'n Charlies. This was a well-known bar and dance club in the heart of Aruba. Natalee would last be seen at approximately 1:30 A.M. on May 30, 2005. The story was only just beginning.

Natalee had met up with locals seemingly every night she went out. Striking up conversations, drinking excessively, and trusting strangers was common by several of the graduates that were there. The last glimpse of Natalee would prove to be the beginning of a complicated, international investigation that would prove nearly impossible to solve. She left the club that morning with 17-year-old Joran van der Sloot, 21-year-old Deepak Kalpoe, and 18-year-old Satish Kalpoe. The events that took place after that are largely contested. Through many different testimonies by witnesses and suspects, investigators would check every lead and run into heartbreaking dead ends.

Upon the morning sunrise, the graduates arrived to board the flight home. It was time to start the rest of their lives. All of the graduates arrived without problem except for one: Natalee Holloway. Through irresponsible chaperoning of a class trip and complete disregard for holding the safety of these students paramount above a fun time, an 18-year-old girl was missing. Her hotel room looked untouched from the previous evening. Her luggage safely packed in anticipation of leaving. No signs of movement in the room. Not even a towel had been disturbed. It was frighteningly clear that she had not returned to her room from the previous night's adventures. When the students and chaperones realized what was going on, they immediately notified authorities. Aruban police initiated immediate searches of the island and its surrounding waters. No trace of her was found.

Joran van der Sloot is undoubtedly the most central figure to this case. Van der Sloot was a 17-year-old Dutch honors student who lived in Aruba. At first glance, his baby face and focused eyes would seemingly make him very approachable to anyone. This was, apparently, not the first night that Natalee and Joran had met. In previous nights, they hung out at bars and engaged in behavior not known to most high school students. Over the course of the next several years, Joran would lead investigators and the Holloway family on a wild goose chase that involved changing alibis, secret videos, and fraud. The innocent appearance that Joran van der Sloot displayed was only a disguise for the true monster he would prove to be.

The Kalpoe brothers were Surinamese friends of van der Sloot. Their significance is much less publicized beyond the last sighting of Holloway. Natalee was last seen getting into Deepak Kalpoe's car with both van der Sloot and Satish. This has been confirmed true by both witnesses and suspects in one way or another. There are numerous stories told by van Sloot and other later suspects that bring the Kalpoe's back to the forefront of the case. In such a complicated investigation, Joran van der Sloot, Deepak Kalpoe, and Satish Kalpoe emerged as early suspects.

Action was fast when news reached family of the mysterious disappearance of Natalee. Her mother, Beth Twitty, immediately boarded a private jet with friends and departed for Aruba. Upon arriving in Aruba, the Twittys had started searching for themselves. They located the Holiday Inn and began asking questions. They had obtained footage from the nightclub she was last seen at. To Beth Twittys surprise, the Holiday Inn workers recognized Joran van der

Sloot instantly. He had apparently been a regular in the area. The helpful Holiday Inn employees provided Beth and company with Joran's name and address. Within a mere four hours since arriving at Aruba, the Twittys had already obtained more information than investigators had been able to. The Twittys provided Aruba Police with this information. It appeared that a case was forming around Van der Sloot already. However, the mishandling of the case and poor techniques of the Aruba Police Department were already rearing their ugly head. This case would prove to be a showcase of poor work, bitter disappointment, and investigators being led around by the suspects themselves. The first lead, however, was officially created.

The Twittys and their friends went to the home of Joran van der Sloot. They were accompanied by two Aruban policemen. The fact that Van der Sloot was even allowed to be approached in this manner showed quickly the lack of thought given to the early stages of the investigation. At this early point in the case, the extent of the crime was largely unknown. Hoping for the best, the Twittys only wished to find Natalee safely at the home of Van der Sloot. Joran answered the door and initially denied even knowing who Natalee Holloway was. After being confronted with evidence of their rendezvous that morning, Van der Sloot admitted to being with Natalee. Also present at the house was Deepak Kalpoe, who was driving the vehicle that Natalee had entered in to.

Van der Sloot gave a sketchy story of what had happened after they left the nightclub. He informed the Twittys as well as the two policemen that they had taken Natalee to the California Lighthouse area. This area was near the nightclub, perhaps a few miles drive depending on the route taken. Natalee had been emphatic that she wanted to see sharks. After leaving the nightclub at 1:30 A.M. they went straight to this area to sight see. Van der Sloot informed them that they had returned Natalee to the Holiday Inn hotel where she had been staying at 2:00 A.M. Natalee, who was heavily intoxicated, stumbled exiting the vehicle. The men had offered to help Natalee to her room, however she refused their help and continued toward the entrance. It was at this time, according to Van der Sloot, that she was approached by a tall man wearing all black. Thinking this was a security guard, the men drove off. This, according to Van der Sloot, was the last interaction of any kind with Natalee Holloway that they had. Deepak Kalpoe affirmed the story and agreed with the events.

This is the initial story of the events. The initial investigation is, perhaps, the most ridiculed part in this case. Not only were the men not detained for further extensive questioning, they were completely presumed to be telling the truth. This not only wasted valuable time in finding Natalee, it also allowed suspects to plan their next move. The fact that Van der Sloot and Kalpoe had initially denied even knowing who Natalee Holloway was should have been the first sign of a problem. The second, and more major sign of a problem would come in the investigation of the hotel surveillance footage. While this was obviously looked at during the investigation, this is largely an accepted procedure that is typically done prior to confronting a potential suspect.

The surveillance footage, or lack thereof, was arguably the single biggest setback with this case. The fact that Natalee was not seen in any hotel footage that fateful morning would lend investigators to believe that Van der Sloot and Kalpoe were lying. The hitch in this was that many statements from the case could not even prove that all cameras were functional at the time. The next problem was the fact that not every entrance had a surveillance. This would leave reasonable doubt that Natalee could have been dropped off near one of these entrances that was simply inaccessible to the surveillance footage.

Investigators finally felt as though they had caught the break in the case they needed when a blood stain was found in Deepak Kalpoe's car. Searching the car that was captured on surveillance as the same one that transported Natalee Holloway from the nightclub, police discovered what appeared to be a blood stain. After lab testing and further investigation, not only was this not Natalee Holloway's blood, it could not even be proven to be blood at all. Another door was closed in the initial investigation of Natalee's disappearance.

After the first full day of investigation, United States involvement in the case began. Monetary assistance was given immediately to aid the Aruban Police Department. Additionally, American searchers sought to help with the advanced search of coastline that had been a constant since Natalee Holloway missed her flight. United States Secretary of State Condoleezza Rice stated "we are in constant contact with Aruban Police. The safe return of Natalee Holloway continues to be our priority."

Hours after missing her flight, the media's involvement in the case was tremendous. All of the major news stations in the United States began their initial coverage of the story. With little facts to go on, it was largely reported as a missing person case with no evidence of foul play. No suspects had truly been pinpointed at this point. The news of her last being seen in the early hours leaving a nightclub led several to assume the worst from the get go, however. It would not be long before Joran van der Sloot was at the fore front of the investigation as well as the ensuing media storm.

It was just six days after Holloway's disappearance that authorities made their first arrest in the case. On June 5, 2005, Abraham Jones and Nick John were placed under arrest. To this day, the exact reasoning behind their arrest is unknown. One of the men had previous encounters with the law, while both were suspected of previously pacing hotels to pick up women. Both men were security guards at a nearby hotel, the Allegro Hotel. It is likely that the statements made by Van der Sloot and Kalpoe led police to this arrest. The men were released on June 13 with no charges being placed. This is yet another example of flawed work by the investigation. It was obvious that police were trusting of Joran van der Sloot and Deepak Kalpoe from the onset. This is a largely debated topic to this day. Many wonder why Van der Sloot and Kalpoe were not arrested initially. However, this was just scratching the surface of what was to come.

On June 9, Joran van der Sloot and both Kalpoe brothers were arrested on suspicion of the kidnapping and murder of Natalee Holloway. In hindsight, it is absolutely unfathomable that it took investigators 10 days to make these arrest. The only evidence they really had at this point was surveillance of Natalee last being seen with these men. Aruban police reported that these men were the "prime suspects from the get-go." While this may have been true to a point, police waited until June 6 to start extended surveillance of the men. Investigators knew they would need much more evidence than a video of Natalee entering a car with the men from the nightclub. Aruban Police instigated phone taps, video surveillance, tailing their vehicles, and monitoring of their e-mails. At this point, in order to continue to hold the three suspects in custody, they would need to provide increasingly substantial evidence at different check points of the investigation. With increasingly consistent pressure from Natalee Holloway's family, police decided to stop the surveillance activities prematurely and execute the arrest on the men.

The arrest of these three suspects was met with heavy interest from people all over the world. The procedures by police and the heavy involvement of the Holloway family seemingly left everyone with an opinion on what should have been conducted differently. Many media outlets focused on the timing of the surveillance activities. Having taken nearly a week to begin the activities from the time of Natalee's last sighting, many felt it was already too late to incriminate the suspects. Also, the fact that surveillance started at the time they had already arrested Adams and John was a bit odd for normal investigative procedure. Lastly, many assumed that if investigators pursued an arrest after just a few days of surveillance of the men, they must have captured something indisputable to implicate one or all of the suspects. This was simply not the case. Aruban Police had missed the initial window of the investigation. Many critics argue that in the interest of uncovering the truth, an extended surveillance would be necessary for the time period they had waited to begin. Investigators instead buckled to pressure from an unorthodox family interaction in a complicated case.

June 11 was the first of many highly publicized false leads. Aruban Minister of Justice David Cruz indicated, in a statement, that Natalee Holloway was dead and that authorities knew the exact location of her body. This was all over most any major media outlet as an early morning breaking news story. The United States was gripped with curiosity and heartbreak as it seemed the terrible truth had come to fruition. Hours later, Cruz released a follow up statement that they had been the victim of "misinformation." This simply is unacceptable. As an investigator or someone in a position as high as Cruz was, you can't put the wagon before the horse, especially to national media outlets. What was the source of this misinformation? Lead investigator Gerold Dompig reported to the Associated Press that one of the detained men had informed them that "something terrible and unthinkable" had happened on the beach after they left the nightclub. The suspect, it was reported, was leading them to the location of the body. This, of course, was another folly.

On June 16, yet another suspect, Steve Gregory Croes, was arrested. "Croes was detained based on urgent information given to us by one of the other three suspect," Aruban Police Superintendent Jan van der Straaten informed the media. While this arrest didn't yield much as far as new leads, it did start to give the appearance that investigators were at a standstill with the case. Six days later on June 22, Joran van der Sloot's father, Paulus, was arrested. This was largely believed to be a bargaining chip to use against Joran. While Paulus was not a suspect, as later revealed by police, he was interrogated in an effort to get more information on Joran. Both Croes and Paulus van der Sloot were released on June 26.

It was around this time where public opinion began to focus on Joran van der Sloot. It was quite clear to all involved that Van der Sloot was not being truthful in his story. The events made little sense to the general public. The longer that Natalee remained missing, the more likely it was that she was, indeed, dead. The suspicion on Joran would only intensify in the coming day.

From the time of the arrest of Joran van der Sloot and the Kalpoe brothers, their stories changed numerous times. In particular, Van der Sloot was giving three completely conflicting stories that would put the focus solely on him.

The first story shift came, oddly enough, from all three suspects. Van der Sloot and both Kalpoe brothers all agreed that Joran and Natalee had been dropped off at the Marriott Hotel beach near several fisherman huts. Van der Sloot was emphatic that he didn't harm Natalee Holloway in any way. He told investigators that they were both heavily intoxicated, and eventually Natalee passed out on the beach. When this happened, he began to walk home. It was at this time that he made a phone call to Deepak Kalpoe that he was walking home. Van der Sloot claims to have sent Kalpoe a text message 40 minutes later. Oddly enough, the phone call nor text message was found in Van der Sloot's phone records.

Lead investigator Gerold Dompig gave insight into the third different story by the suspects. This story, told by Joran van der Sloot, was a turning point in that it showed that he was willing to change his story however he saw fit in order to avoid suspicion.

"The latest story came when Joran saw that his buddies, the Kalpoe's, were essentially pointing the finger in his direction. He wanted to screw them by pointing the finger right back at them. But the story simply doesn't check out. He just wanted to screw Deepak. They (Deepak and Joran) had great arguments about this in front of the judge. Their stories didn't match. Joran felt the focus shifting to him and was willing to do anything to change it. That girl, she was from

Alabama. She is not going to stay in the car with two black kids while Joran simply gets out of the car to head home alone. We firmly believe the second story; that they were dropped off at the Marriott. This goes along with the timeline and the stories given by the Kalpoe's."

Upon hearings in front of the judge on July 4, both Satish and Deepak Kalpoe were released from custody. Joran van der Sloot was to remain for a minimum of 60 days. Focus was solely on Van der Sloot as the main suspect in the disappearance of Natalee Holloway.

For nearly all of July, searches for Natalee Holloway remained fruitless endeavors. Investigators had no leads and were consistently getting varied stories from Joran van der Sloot. While police had solid suspicions of Van der Sloot, they had essentially zero solid evidence against him. The media storm updated the world daily on search efforts. With each passing day, reality began to set in for many that Natalee Holloway may never be found. Initially, a $50,000 reward was offered for Natalee's safe return. On July 25, the reward for the safe return of Holloway had increased all the way to $1,000,000. In addition, a $100,000 reward was offered for information that would lead to the location of her remains. In August of the same year, the reward for the location of her remains would raise all the way to $250,000. This was widely covered by the media and many local and national governments. This was a final attempt by investigators to break the cold case open. This strategy had several negative impacts, however. The most severe of these were the wasted time on false leads and folly calls. This was not anticipated by investigators as it should have been.

Between July 27 and 30, investigators initiated a massive undertaking. The pond in front of the Aruba Racquet Club was completely drained. This was within one mile of the Marriott Hotel where Van der Sloot had apparently taken Natalee Holloway. A tip was given to police that was especially unique. A gardener had apparently seen Joran van der Sloot driving into the Racquet Club with the Kalpoe brothers. Van der Sloot was said to have been hiding his face. The gardener informed police that the men were seen driving in between 2:30 A.M. and 3:00 A.M. on the morning of May 30. The search of the pond bed and surrounding area, however, yielded no clues.

On July 28, a jogger came forward with a frightening testimony. The United States media covered this story heavily for several days as it was the first story of someone seeing a woman resembling Natalee Holloway since her disappearance. The jogger claimed that she saw a group of men burying a young, blonde haired woman on the afternoon of May 30 at a landfill. The landfill was subsequently searched three separate times with precision. This search, again, yielded no results.

In late August, Joran van der Sloot became the front page villain to many. Throughout the entire case, it was well covered as to how many variations of a story Joran had given. While showing no remorse or empathy for the Holloway family, the public formed a very negative opinion of Van der Sloot. Anita van der Sloot would provide more material for the family. "It's a desperate attempt to get the boys to talk. But there is nothing to talk about. Joran has no fault in this mystery." Joran van der Sloot's mother made this statement after police again brought in the Kalpoe's for questioning. This left a bitter taste in the mouths of many. It was shaping up to be Van der Sloot's versus investigators.

On September 3, 2005, Joran van der Sloot was released from custody due to insufficient evidence to hold. By September 14, all restrictions were officially lifted from Van der Sloot. Whatever the events of May 30, no suspect was in custody and there were no leads for police. Joran van der Sloot was a free man. The release of Van der Sloot created a frenzy among the general public. People all over the United States and surrounding areas were furious, set in their beliefs that a guilty man was walking away free. The nation was gripped against a common villain.

The months that followed Joran van der Sloot's release provided media cannon fodder of epic proportions. Van der Sloot did several interviews and even composed a book of his take on the events of the night. To the public's astonishment, this man was now profiting off of this whole fire storm of a case. The most notable post release interview came with Fox News on a three night special. Van der Sloot claims that the two were heavily intoxicated on the beach after leaving the nightclub. He went into great detail about the two planning an escapade on the beach, narcotic use, and partying in a fun filled night in Aruba. He showed little empathy or remorse for any of the events. He seemingly talked about Natalee as if she was the villain. Joran went on to explain that Natalee wanted to have sex on the beach, however he didn't have a condom. He left her on the beach and was driven home by Satish Kalpoe. Later, Satish Kalpoe's lawyer claims that Satish was asleep well before this would have happened. Joran went on to explain that he was embarrassed for having left a beautiful woman alone on the beach, citing this as the reason for his ever changing story. He said that he was convinced Holloway would turn up.

This all sat so negatively to viewers. There was outrage over the handling of the investigation. People could not understand how no evidence existed to implicate a man that was deemed the perpetrator. Aruba authorities later claimed that over $3 million had been spent on the investigation. This was over 40% of the overall budget for investigative expenditures.

On December 18, 2007 after extensive efforts to implicate the Kalpoe brothers and/or Joran van der Sloot, the case was officially closed. Prosecutors cited lack of evidence to a violent crime, lack of evidence to a murder, as well as lack of continued funding for the expensive investigation. Over two full years after the disappearance of Natalee Holloway, the case was closed. The remains of Natalee Holloway had not been found. Joran van der Sloot not only was a free man, but had profited greatly from the publicity of the case. This, however, would not be the final chapter to the journey of Joran van der Sloot.

In the years after the closing of the Natalee Holloway case, Joran van der Sloot told several variations of events of that fateful morning. He gave countless interviews, seemingly telling a different story in each one of them. Ultimately, Joran van der Sloot was seeking money and fame through his disgusting actions. In an interview with Fox News in 2008, he claimed to have sold Natalee Holloway in sexual slavery. He later retracted the statements in the days after. It was reported in 2010 that in a 2009 interview with RTL group, he claimed he disposed of the body in a marsh area in Aruba. This interview was never confirmed, nor denied by investigators or Van der Sloot.

Remarkably, Van der Sloot would show his greed had no limits. On March 29, 2010 Van der Sloot contacted Beth Twittys legal representative. He offered to give the location to Natalee Holloway's remains in exchange for $25,000. After contacting police, the transaction was made. $15,000 was wired to Van der Sloot's account, and the remaining $10,000 was given by a middle man. The receipt of the transaction was videotaped by police. The information provided by Van der Sloot was proven false, as the building that he claimed housed the remains was not yet built at the time of the disappearance. Van der Sloot would be indicted on June 30 of the same year. However, he was about to be indicted for a much more serious crime.

On May 30, 2010, exactly five years from the time of the disappearance of Natalee Holloway, Stephany Flores Ramirez was reported missing in Lima, Peru. Ironically, she was found dead just three days later in a hotel room registered to Joran van der Sloot. On June 7, 2010, Van der Sloot confessed to killing Ramirez after he lost his temper while she was using his laptop. Within the same interview, he said that he knew where Holloway's body was. Dealing with jurisdiction issues, Peruvian police could not further investigate the Holloway statement without Aruban authorities.

Aruban authorities were granted interrogation of Van der Sloot in Peru in June of 2010. While he would not confess to murdering

Holloway or her whereabouts, he did admit to the extortion plot on the Holloway family. "I wanted to get back at Natalee's family. They have been making my life miserable for the last five years," Van der Sloot said. Van der Sloot was found guilty in the murder of Stephany Flores Ramirez and sentenced to 28 years in prison. This sentence also included his time for his extortion of the Holloway family.

Natalee Holloway's remains have never been found. There have never been any convictions made into the disappearance of Natalee or any criminal wrong doing. In this case, it would be naïve to imagine a scenario where Joran van der Sloot was not responsible in some way for the death of Natalee Holloway. While Van der Sloot waste the best years of his life behind bars, a young woman with an extremely bright future is still gone. Closure will never be possible for the Holloway family. Perhaps a poor investigative strategy is to blame for the lack of any convictions. Maybe it is the irresponsible planning of school personnel and behavior supervision by chaperones could have prevented this tragedy. Better decision by Natalee herself may have helped avoid such a terrible event. In any case, an intelligent young woman who had everything in front of her did not deserve this end. The Holloway family did not deserve this. We will likely never know the true events of that fateful May morning. What we do know is that we will never get to see the true potential that Natalee Holloway had.

FINDING JENNIFER : THE DISAPPEARANCE OF JENNIFER KESSE

MARY DANIELLE TAYLOR

The unsolved disappearance of Jennifer Kesse from her Orlando, Florida condo in the early hours of January 23, 2006, garnered widespread attention from the local and national media alike, leading to large-scale search parties conducted by the Orlando Police Department and FBI. However, despite the fact that Jennifer Kesse disappeared over ten years ago in the parking lot of her apartment complex, investigators are no closer to solving the case.

Jennifer Kesse, a finance manager for a Florida property and vacation company, had left her recently purchased condo in Orlando, Florida to begin her morning commute to work. However, Jennifer would never make it into work that morning, and her family and friends would never hear from her again. Read on to learn more about who Jennifer Kesse was, about the circumstances of her disappearance, and the local and national reaction to her missing persons case.

Early Life

Jennifer Kesse, a graduate of Vivian Gaither High School in Tampa, Florida, had graduated with a degree in finance from the University of Central Florida, located in Orlando, Florida, in 2003, where she also served as a member of the Alpha Delta Pi sorority. Following her graduation from college, Jennifer began working at the Central Florida Investments Timeshare Company as a finance manager.

Shortly before the date of her disappearance, Jennifer and her current boyfriend had visited Saint Croix, in the U.S. Virgin Islands, for a vacation. After returning home from the Virgin Islands by plane, Jennifer drove directly from her boyfriend's house in South Florida to her job in Ocoee, Florida for a full day of work. Jennifer would return home to her newly-purchased condo in Orlando that evening, the very same evening of her disappearance.

Night of Her Disappearance

Jennifer was last seen leaving the Westgate Resorts office of the Central Florida Investments Timeshare Company on the night of

January 23, 2006 in Ocoee, Florida, after returning home from her vacation in Saint Croix, in the U.S. Virgin Islands, with her boyfriend. Several close friends and members of her family received calls from Jennifer that night, and the last call that she made before her disappearance was to her boyfriend shortly before 10:00pm.

Jennifer typically called or texted her boyfriend during her morning commute to work to wish him good morning; however, he became concerned on the morning of January 24th when he did not receive a message from her. When he attempted to call Jennifer that morning, his call was sent directly to voicemail. Because Jennifer had previously told him that she had an early-morning meeting at work, he assumed that she was busy and would call him once she received his voicemail. He continued his day at work until receiving a call from Jennifer's parents later that day informing him that she had never made it to work.

When Jennifer did not show up to work or contact her direct supervisor, a coworker contacted Jennifer's parents to express concern and see if they had heard from her. Jennifer was supposed to attend a very important work meeting with her higher-ups that morning, and it was extremely unlike her to fail to show up with calling ahead. Upon receiving the call from Jennifer's office, her parents immediately jumped into action. Her father, Drew Kesse, said "We were calling hospitals, calling jails, calling her friends, asking them to call places, calling Rob, and he tried calling her and she did not answer."

Her parents soon jumped into their car and made the two-hour drive to Jennifer's condo in Orlando, Florida from their home in Tampa. While driving, her parents contact her condo management office at *Mosaic Apartments*, located on the 3700 block Convoy Road in Orlando, and requested that the manager stop by her condo to check on her. He reported that she was not home, that her condo was in great condition, and that her car was not in the parking lot.

In addition, once her parents arrived in Orlando and entered their daughter's condo, they did not notice anything out of place or any signs of a struggle. Furthermore, they noticed that Jennifer's clothes were laid out on her bed and that a wet towel was present in the restroom, leading them to believe that Jennifer was at home that morning. Her father Drew later said, "We actually found two or three outfits laid out on her bed she was picking. Showered, shower was still damp. Her towel was still damp. Her work stuff was not there. So we knew that, OK, she got ready for work."

The parents quickly contacted the Orlando police department to report her as missing. Family members began passing out flyers that evening and reaching out to local media organizations, while the local police department began organizing a search party.

A local television reporter and friend of Jennifer's, Scott Thuman, described the family's actions like this: "I made sure they were on every TV station every single night as long as we could keep that alive. They did the networks, they did radio shows. They did every newspaper interview they could." An investigative reporter who covered the case would later say, "It was hard to go anywhere without seeing her face and her picture and also the information on her vehicle."

Timeline

<u>January 23, 2006</u>

Early Morning – Leaves her boyfriend's home in Central Florida to head directly to her office at Westgate Resorts for a full day at work. Jennifer and her boyfriend had just returned from a trip to Saint Croix, U.S. Virgin Islands.

6:00pm – Jennifer leaves her office at Westgate Resorts and drives to her condo complex in Orlando, Fiolrida. She unpacks her clothes and contacts several family members to let them know that she has returned home from vacation safely.

10:00pm – Jennifer calls her boyfriend and speaks with him for several minutes before saying goodnight. Jennifer's boyfriend is the last known person to speak with her before her disappearance.

January 24, 2006

7:30am – Police believe that Jennifer was abducted sometime around 7:30am to 8:00am on the morning of the 24th. She was likely taken either while walking through the parking lot towards her car or while entering her vehicle.

8:30am – Jennifer's boyfriend calls her, but the call is sent directly to voicemail. Jennifer typically calls her boyfriend during her morning commute to say good morning and chat. He assumes that she is busy with an early-morning meeting that they had previously discussed.

11:00am – Jennifer's coworkers, concerned that she uncharacteristically did not show up to work and had missed a very important meeting, called her parents to see if Jennifer is okay. Both her parents and coworkers realize that something is wrong.

11:15am – Jennifer's parents immediately begin the two-hour drive to Jennifer's condo in Orlando from their home in Tampa. Her parents contact her condo's management office and request that they enter her condo to check on her. He reports that nothing is out of the ordinary and that her car is gone.

12:00pm – Jennifer's brother, who lives locally, arrives at her condo complex and begins looking for her. Unbeknownst to anyone at the time, a surveillance camera at an apartment complex 1 mile down the road from her own condo shows an unidentifiable man parking Jennifer's car. The video shows the suspect parking the car, and sitting in it for approximately 30 seconds before exiting the car and walking away from the complex. Unfortunately for investigators, the suspect's face was obscured by a fencing post and neither the local police department nor the FBI were able to produce a useable shot of the suspect's face.

1:00pm – Jennifer's parents arrive in Orlando and immediately enter her condo. They notice that her shower is covered with water and that her towel is still wet. They also see that her work clothes are laid out on her unmade bed, that her makeup and hairdryer are lying out on her bathroom sink, and that her pajamas are piled on the restroom floor. Police theorize that Jennifer may have had a fight with her boyfriend and left her apartment to cool off. They preach patience to the parents.

5:00pm – Jennifer's close family and friends begin passing out missing persons flyers to local passerby. The police respond by sending a detective to her condo to gather information and investigate her disappearance. Police begin to question her family and friends, and begin to organize a search party.

<u>January 26, 2006</u>

8:10am – After seeing a report on Jennifer's disappearance on the local news, a resident at a local apartment complex calls the Orlando Police Department to report that her car has been parked in their complex for the last two days. Police arrive at the complex to verify this report, and quickly haul the car away to local police facilities for a forensic analysis. Police are finally able to identify and locate security footage showing an unidentified person parking Jennifer's car and leaving the complex by foot. This footage would lead investigators to determine that Jennifer may have been abducted.

Investigation

Jennifer's parents, as well as the initial investigators who looked into her case, noticed that Jennifer's apartment showed no signs of forced entry, her condo door was locked, and there were no signs of a struggle. Furthermore, because Jennifer's work clothes were laid out neatly and there was evidence that she had recently showered, investigators theorized that she had gotten ready for work the morning of her disappearance and had left her condo to begin her morning commute. The also assert that Jennifer likely left her apartment and was abducted either during the walk to her car or as she was entering the vehicle.

Two days after Jennifer's disappearance on January 26th, her 2004 black Chevy Malibu was located at the *Huntington on the Green* apartment complex, located at Americana Ave. and Texas, a little over a mile away from her own condo. While the apartment complex her car was parked at did have several security cameras, covering both her car and the exit to the apartment complex itself, the videos offered limited clues to her disappearance.

The video showed a "person of interest" who dropped off her car at noon the day of her disappearance; however, the best shots from the video were rendered useless since fencing from the apartment complex concealed the face of the unidentified man in three separate frames. The suspect was seen wearing an all-white uniform, leading some close to the case to believe that the suspect was a painter or other type of manual laborer.

Beau Zimmer, an investigative reporter who followed Jennifer Kesse's disappearance, described the video like this: "There's two different angles, all surrounding the pool area. But it's very, very blurry and it's hard to see. But you can see someone pulling Jennifer's car into that visitor's parking lot. They wait inside the car for a number of seconds before they get out and look around, and then walk out of frame of the picture. But the next shot of the video was what everyone thought would be so helpful. The next shot was of a person that was walking back and forth along the fence line."

However, he noted, "Every frame of the video, the person is obscured by a post and so you never see the person's face." Zimmer would later remark, "It has got to be the most frustrating thing for detectives, the most frustrating thing for the Kesse family, because for just one split second, later or earlier, you would have seen that individual's face and you would have had a better idea of what happened to Jennifer."

When investigators shared footage from the video with Jennifer's family and friends, they were unable to identify the man in question. A Fox News reporter would later say in a televised retrospective segment on the case that the obscured image made the man the "luckiest person of interest ever."

Both the FBI and NASA were called in to conduct advanced video analyses of the footage to provide more clues on the stalled case. The FBI determined that the person was roughly 5'3" to 5'5" tall, but could not offer definitive proof of the suspect's gender. Despite NASA's digital enhancement of the video, they were not able to provide any additional information that could help the case.

Despite the dead-end that the surveillance video represented, investigators were able to put together several pieces of the puzzle. Since all of Jennifer's valuables were found in her car, parked a mile down the street in a different apartment complex, they were able to determine that robbery was not a primary motive in her disappearance. In addition, a police dog was able to track a scent a full mile from her parked car back to her condo complex, leading investigators to theorize that the unidentified suspect returned to her complex directly after disposing of her car. However, police were unable to locate any helpful evidence along the route walked by the suspect.

After conducted a search and forensic analysis of her vehicle, investigators identified two pieces of evidence: a latent fingerprint from an unidentified individual and a small strand of DNA. Given the lack of evidence found in the car, coupled with the lack of clothing fibers, hair strands, and DNA, the police believe that the car was thoroughly wiped down in an attempt to remove incriminating evidence. The investigative reporter assigned to the case, Beau Zimmer, would say, "There was maybe one print and detectives think that it was maybe wiped down, and that this was an intentional act to not only hide this vehicle, but also to hide any evidence of who may have driven it."

Despite the lack of evidence found in her car, investigators did notice that several items were missing. They were unable to located her cell phone, keys, purse, clothes, briefcase, or iPod. While police are often able to track a missing person's cell phone or bank accounts for clues, her bank account was never accessed by her captors and her cell phone remained turned off with the battery removed.

Investigators quickly compiled a list of potential suspects after questioning her friends and family for clues. Her current boyfriend was questioned and quickly eliminated from the list of suspects after providing a valid alibi. In addition, Jennifer's ex-boyfriend and one of her coworkers, who had romantic feelings for Jennifer and had sought a relationship with her in the past, were interviewed by the police.

One the of the most interesting factors in Jennifer's disappearance was the fact that her condo complex was undergoing major construction at the time of her disappearance. Many of the workers, some who were undocumented immigrants, were living in the complex while it was undergoing construction. Jennifer had mentioned her discomfort with some of the workers to her family on multiple occasions, claiming that they harassed and catcalled her regularly. Jennifer's parents have also stated on multiple occasions that they believe she may have been a victim of human trafficking.

In May 2007, the CEO of Central Florida Investments Timeshare Company, David Siegel, offered a $1 million reward for information that led to her being found alive; however, the reward was never claimed. A $5,000 reward for information on her disappearance, offered by the Central Florida Crime line, remains active today.

Suspects

Ex-boyfriend

Jennifer had recently broken up with a previous boyfriend, and he was reportedly very angry about the breakup and the fact that Jennifer was now dating another man. Beau Zimmer would report that Jennifer's ex-boyfriend became incredibly angry after finding out that she was travelling to Saint Croix with Rob, saying "The night before or sometime before, he had been out drinking and gotten drunk and apparently he was upset that he was not the one that was with Jennifer.

Zimmer would later remark that the ex-boyfriend was cleared by the police, saying "They talked with him several times, and while police say he is not a suspect in the case, certainly you get the feeling from others that he should be talked to a little bit more."

Current Boyfriend

Jennifer's boyfriend, Rob, was initially considered a suspect in her disappearance. The couple had just returned from a vacation in Saint Croix, in the U.S. Virgin Islands, and Rob was the last person who had spoken with Jennifer the night before her disappearance. Police soon interviewed Rob to learn more about his relationship with Jennifer and to ascertain his whereabouts the morning of her disappearance.

However, Rob was quickly discounted as a suspected. Rob had an airtight alibi; he was more than 200 miles away when Jennifer was abducted, at his home in Fort Lauderdale, Florida. Investigative journalist Beau Zimmer says, "The police said that between his phone records and the fact that he was in South Florida, we don't believe that he was involved."

The police department's belief in Rob's innocence is shared by Jennifer's family. He was fully cooperative with the police department and FBI's investigation and willingly provided a DNA sample twice. Jennifer's father, Drew Kesse, said "Rob has been put over the coals, Rob has been polygraphed three of four times, Rob has been interviewed probably over a dozen times."

Coworker

Both Jennifer's family, friends, and coworkers reported that Jennifer had recently turned down a coworker who was hitting on her and attempting to strike up a romantic relationship. Jennifer's mom, Joyce, said that the coworker was married and was refusing to accept Jennifer's decision not to date him, both because he was married and because she did not date people she worked with. Joyce later said, "Jennifer arranged to meet him in the cafeteria at work so that once and for all she could tell him, 'Leave me alone, I am never going to date you. And besides, I don't date married men.'"

The police department did question Jennifer's coworker and eventually eliminated him from the list of suspects. However, Joyce said "We feel it should have been consistent to keep the pressure on that individual."

Construction Workers

Jennifer, who had just purchased and moved into her newly renovated condo two months before her disappearance, had repeatedly expressed concern about construction workers in her complex. The complex, which was undergoing extensive renovations at the time, was housing undocumented immigrants working on the consecution projects, at the time of her disappearance. Beau Zimmer has stated, "Jennifer told some of her friends that she felt really uncomfortable around some of these guys. Apparently there may have been some cat calls and things like that."

Jennifer's parents have also stated that she may have been abducted by a construction worker, with her mother saying, "I can't help wonder if someone was stalking her from afar that she didn't even know. Could there have been someone watching her comings and goings?"

The local police department did question many of the construction workers who were working at her condo complex at the time of her disappearance; however, no leads would develop from this line of questioning. Zimmer would say, "The police tried to talk to as many of the workers that would have been there when Jennifer disappeared, but they acknowledge that they may have missed some people."

Sex Traffickers

Drew Kesse has claimed that it is well-known that there was an active sex trafficking ring in the Orlando area at the time of Jennifer's disappearance, which her parents think may be linked to her abduction. Jennifer's father, Drew Kesse, has stated "My gut feeling to this day, honestly, I truly believe she was trafficked." His sentiment was echoed by Jennifer's close friend and local television reporter Scott Thuman, was said "It would make sense on a lot of levels, as unfortunate as it is."

Reaction

The disappearance of Jennifer Kesse led to nationwide outrage and attention, with coverage in the local, state, national, and international media. At the behest of Orlando Police Department chief Val Demings, the FBI took over control of the case on June 10, 2010 and remains in-charge of her missing persons case to this day. She remains on the FBI's Missing List and they continue to search for her and react to current leads, with the most recent search taking place in February 2014. She is also still considered still missing by the Orlando Police Department, Interpol, and the Orange County, Florida Police Department.

In reaction to Jennifer's disappearance and the investigation into her disappearance. The Florida House of Representatives passed Senate Bill 502, entitled "The Jennifer Kesse and Tiffany Sessions Missing Persons Act," by unanimous vote on May 2, 2008. This bill changed the way that missing persons cases are handled in the state of Florida, instituting reforms such as allowing the Florida Department of Law Enforcement to provide assistance in missing persons cases involving adults. Prior to the passage of this law, the FDLE was limited in its ability to provide assistance in cases involving the disappearance or abduction of adults aged 26 or older.

THE DISAPPEARANCE OF TARA CALICO

91

NICK PESCI

<u>Tara Calico Mystery</u>

The story of Tara Calico is one of confusion, uncertainty, and sadness. The events of her disappearance are one of the least understood of any crime over the past 50 years. A single Polaroid showing what is widely believed to be Tara, ultimately gives her disappearance its most notable name: The Polaroid Mystery.

Tara Calico was born on February 28, 1969 to loving parents in New Mexico. She led the typical American childhood. She had a huge amount of friends and extended family. Many were drawn to her bright personality and contagious smile. Even at an early age, she was developing into a tall, athletic young woman. She took a great interest in sports and outdoor activities. Among her favorite things to do was biking, hiking, and camping.

Tara Calico succeeded greatly in school. She had a strong interest in most every subject. Her parents would describe her as "the sweetest girl who never wanted to get in trouble". She had earned an opportunity to continue her education at the University of New Mexico at Valencia.

She had also formed a strong relationship with her boyfriend around the time she turned 18 years old. The two were seemingly a perfect match. Instead of movies and dinners, this couple preferred biking and walking, most any activity that required physical activity. Tara's parents enjoyed seeing her so happy. When she was just 19 years old, however, things would change forever.

On the morning of September 20, 1988 everything would change for Tara and her family. She was in a joyful mood. She was enjoying a day off from school at her family home in Belen, New Mexico. The weather was perfect. It was a mild morning and a great climate to get out and enjoy the day. Tara was an avid biker. She decided to embark on a long, 17 mile bike route that would ultimately lead to her returning back to her home in Belen.

She planned to leave at 9:30 A.M. The route she would take would make an elaborate oval that would take her around the railroad tracks as well as the Rio Communities Golf Course. The route had some definite scenic areas, especially the trail along the railroad tracks. The beautiful weather meant that she would be able to make great time on the trip.

She had a lunch date with her boyfriend for noon. The couple planned to play tennis that afternoon. She had made a phone call to her boyfriend that morning and everything was completely normal. Looking back at the entire event, there was one thing that eerily stood out to her family. Before Tara left for her bike ride, she had told her mother jokingly that "if she wasn't back by noon, to come look for her." This was meant to be a playful banter between Tara and her mother, but ultimately could not have been any truer. This was the ultimate, real life foreshadowing that would turn out to be such a nightmare for all involved. Upon leaving for her bike ride at 9:30 A.M. she made her statement and rode off into the gorgeous morning air. This would be the last time anyone would see her alive in person.

Noon approached, and passed. Tara's mother became a bit anxious at the whole situation. Specifically, Tara was not one to arrive late or not show up when she was supposed to. All her mother could think of was the grim last words she had been told by Tara. As 12:30 P.M. approached, Patty Doel, Tara's mother, decided to look along the route she had taken to quell her worries. At this point, Patty felt it was likely that Tara was just running behind or maybe even stopped to enjoy the beautiful day. All that being said, Patty got in her car and went out to search along the route.

Patty got in her car and headed south on N.M. 47. This led to the Rio Communities where she would spend the majority of her trek. Seeing no sign of Tara in the least, full panic began to set in for Patty. Perhaps she had taken an alternate route or had merely stopped to see a friend. As it approached 1:00 P.M. Patty knew something was wrong. A strong sense of uneasiness came over Patty Doel. Something just wasn't right. By this time, she had missed her tennis date with her boyfriend and was entirely too late to assume that she had just been riding at a slow pace. Tara was a teenager who rode her bike religiously. A 17 mile ride would not take near this long, especially with a known route that she had used many times before. Something was terribly wrong, and it was up to Patty to figure out what that may be.

Patty continued to circle the roads around the Rio Communities. She decided it may be best to creep along the shoulder of the road in an attempt to see into the ditches. Maybe Tara had an accident and was stuck in the ditch. What Patty would find would confirm her worst fear.

Patty Doel froze as she saw something laying on the side of the road. It was a Boston cassette tape.

Tara Calico was a typical teenage girl for the time as she loved music. She was a huge fan of Boston. Most any bike ride that Tara would take would feature a water bottle, helmet, and her Sony Walkman. Most often, she would be listening to Boston.

The morning of September 20 was no different. She had her water bottle, helmet, and her Sony Walkman. She had a Boston cassette tape to accompany her on her long bike ride that morning.

As Patty approached the cassette tape and noticed that it was Boston, she lost all control of her worries. She knew in her heart that something was terribly wrong. Patty Doel immediately called police.

An expansive search of the area followed. Police questioned her family to get a sense of any possible place she could have went. Investigators initially believed that she was likely at a friend's house and failed to notify her mother. After all, she was a 19 year old college student. She easily could have felt that it was not necessary to notify her mother of minor changes to her day like this. Patty knew better. Patty suspected foul play. She also felt that Tara was smart enough to have left the Boston cassette as a clue to investigators and her mother that something wasn't right.

All those that were interviewed agreed that Tara was not the kind to vanish without notifying those around her. She had never done anything like that before, and she had no reason to have done it then. Her boyfriend agreed, citing that she had never missed a date they had scheduled and would never "stand him up", especially for an activity such as tennis or anything else physical. At this point, full panic mode had been reached by everyone who was at all close to Tara. It was now a race against the clock.

At this point, police were quite skeptical of the entire situation. A Boston cassette on the side of the road and a 19 year old woman who was late returning home was, in their mind, just simply not enough to conduct a full missing person report. After all, there were thousands of Boston cassette, presumably, in the area. If a missing person report and search was filed each time a 19 year old was late coming home, then there would be hundreds of such reports each day.

Everything changed for police later that day. A policeman spotted a pink Huffy bicycle in a ditch along with a Sony Walkman roughly 20 miles from the home of Tara Calico. This changed everything. Police were now as convinced as Tara's family that something substantial had happened to her. Her bicycle, Walkman, and Boston cassette found thrown in the ditch caught their attention. Moreover, the location of the bicycle being so far from the home alerted police that she had either been taken from this location, or perhaps had been taken closer to her home and the bike and Walkman were simply thrown out at this point. Either way, investigators knew they had a major problem on their hands. They also knew that time was of utter importance if there was any hope to find Tara alive. They would need to work fast and efficiently.

New Mexico detectives began to put all of their resources to this case. They questioned anyone around the seen and interviewed hundreds of people. Being as the route that Tara was to take was so long, they felt confident that someone, somewhere saw something of importance that may lead to a break in the case. Several people confirmed that a 1953 Ford F-150 pickup truck had been seen following Tara just a few miles from her house. This truck had an attached camper shell on it, which would prove significant. It was not known if Tara Calico knew who these people were, or even if she was aware someone was behind her. After all, she had music blaring in her ears from her Walkman which likely would have made it impossible for her to hear anything behind her.

Investigators felt it was significant to understand a bit about the social aspect of Tara. Tara Calico was a tall, athletic young woman who anyone would say was an attractive woman. There were many men who wanted to be with her and date her, and she was vocal to her friends about how she was approached many times by men asking her out. Her boyfriend affirmed this, as he said men had even approached her when they were together. Investigators thought this was significant for two reasons. First, Tara may very well have known who these people were. If she knew who was in the F-150, she may have simply been ignoring them and continuing on her route. Second, Tara may not have understood the present danger by strangers approaching her. After all, she had been approached on numerous occasions by strangers and may have just chalked it up to another guy trying to get a date with her. All in all, police could neither prove nor support these theories without more evidence. Finding a motive or a reason in an effort to gain a lead would prove near impossible.

Even with extensive investigation by New Mexico police, the case really had no lead. The 1953 Ford F-150 was searched for in the area. However, it was not found. Tara Calico was proven to be on the bike trails and the streets around the trails on her 17 mile route. It was also confirmed that her bike and Sony Walkman were those that were found by police on the day of her disappearance. With eye witness testimony and her last known activity before her disappearance, police had nothing at all to work on for the case. She had seemingly disappeared without a trace beyond her bike and Walkman. The case ran cold for almost a year. Posters were put out, local news showed her picture and garnered attention to a hotline number for information on whereabouts. Family members urged anyone who knew anything suspicious to come forward. Rewards were offered by police and family members alike. There just weren't any leads in the case. Life would drag along for the family of Tara and her boyfriend, who was actually a suspect early in the case as police searched for answers. The whole situation was a sad reminder that closure may not come in this case, and that Tara may never be found alive. What started as a beautiful day that was perfect for a bike ride, turned into the worst nightmare for all of those involved. Police, however, finally caught a break in the most unlikely of cases. What would be discovered would be the single piece of evidence that would put this case on a national stage, and would ultimately give the case its name.

As the months dragged on, few within the family of Tara Calico thought any answers would arrive. In June of 1989, a break in the case would come. The harsh reality of this break, however, was that it would bring about many more questions with fewer answers.

It was a blistering summer for most all of the United States. In Port St. Joe, Florida, the heat was at an extreme. In this unlikely place, the name of Tara Calico would be brought to the forefront.

Port St. Joe Florida is just over 1,600 miles away from Belen, New Mexico. The story of Tara Calico had been scarcely seen in this distant place. On a June afternoon, nearly 9 full months since Tara Calico disappeared from Belen, New Mexico, a woman came upon something on the ground in a grocery store parking lot that caught her eye. As she walked closer to the strange object laying on the ground, she discovered it to be a single Polaroid photograph. This obviously peaked her curiosity. She decided that she would pick this photograph up. The striking image she would discover would open the case of Tara Calico up in a way never imagined.

The photograph showed a grave image. There were two people in the photograph. One of the people was a teenage woman, the other, a young boy, perhaps around ten years old. Both of them had black tape covering their mouths, not wrapped all the way around the head but just about ear to ear across the mouth. Each of them had their hands seemingly tied behind their backs, although the hands are out of picture so any further information on this is solely based on assumption. The woman is tall, having very long legs and a slight discoloration on the right calf, appearing to be a scar of some sort. She is wearing black gym style shorts with a grey t-shirt. She has dark colored hair that is pulled back behind her head. Nearly her whole body is visible in the photograph. The boy is in the background angle of the photograph. He is much younger than the female in the picture, and he too has black tape over his mouth in the same manner. His hands are also behind his back, assumed to be tied up. He is wearing a light blue t-shirt.

The face of each of them tell a story. The look of fear is much more present on the young boys face. They look tired and confused and are both staring directly at the camera.

The photo appears to have been taken in the back of a van of some sort. Both of the apprehended people are on blankets and pillows lying down with their heads against the side of the structure. The background is dark, creating an image that appears to have no light directly in their area, rather light that is coming in from the front of the structure behind the person taking the photograph.

In the bottom left corner of the photograph is a book. The book titled *My Sweet Andria* was written by V.C. Andrews. This would prove to be a key clue to investigators.

The woman quickly turned in the photograph to authorities. Upon investigation of the area, witnesses reported that a white Toyota cargo van had been parked in the area that morning. The van nor the driver were ever located. Witnesses described the driver of the van to be in his 30's with a thick handlebar style mustache. He was reported to be slender and of extremely fair complexion. He would never be located officially by investigators.

Investigators quickly noticed a striking resemblance to Tara Calico. Patty Doel was brought in to study the photograph and was convinced that it was Tara. Upon close review and a bit of background on Tara, she had strong reason to believe so.

The woman in the Polaroid was tall, athletic, and very slender toned. This matched Tara exactly. The hair color matched as well as the facial features and shape. The scar on the right leg of the woman in the photograph was also a chilling resemblance to one that Tara had. These clues in themselves were enough to safely attest that the girl in the photograph was, in fact, Tara Calico.

In addition to the physical features of the woman in the photograph was the odd placement of the book next to her. The book was written by V.C. Andrews, which was oddly enough the favorite author of Tara. She had read all of the V.C. Andrews books and was an avid reader. This, to many investigators and to Patty Doel, was the final piece of evidence to prove that the woman in the photograph was Tara Calico. But who was the boy in the photograph?

The young boy in the Polaroid appeared to be between 9 and 11 years old. Investigators initially believed the young boy to be Michael Henley. Michael went missing in April of 1988 in Zunis Mountain, New Mexico. He was camping with his family when he wandered off and never returned to the campsite. This would make the most sense to investigators as is would explain why Tara Calico was in the photograph as well. Both of the victims would have been assumed to have been taken from the same area around the same time.

In 1990, however, Michael Henley's remains were found just a few miles from the area that the family had been camping. It was determined that he died from exposure to the elements after presumably becoming lost in the wilderness of the area and not being able to find his way back. This was a turning point in the case as it raised doubts in the investigators minds as to the true identity of the people in the photograph.

Another problem that investigators had with the photograph was the legitimacy of the photo itself. Several people claimed that the Polaroid appeared staged. While this is a grim thought that is a terrible thing to assume, it was in fact a reality of the times. Singer Marilyn Manson famously set photos similar to this out randomly in this area as a prank. Most investigators, however, felt this photo was legitimate and not in any way staged.

Joel Nugent believed the photo to be entirely genuine. Joel Nugent was the lead investigator of the Florida case as a part of the Gulf County Sheriff's Department.

"It obviously is two kids with terror written all over them. It's kind of a bad time when you have to look at something like that and wonder. No one knows for sure if the picture was a setup. Some people think it was a stage photograph, but it was a real look of fear for me."

On September 20, 1989 *Unsolved Mysteries* aired a special on the Tara Calico disappearance. It marked the one year anniversary of her disappearance. Months prior, in July 1989, a special on Tara was aired on *A Current Affair*. Additionally, as the months turned into years, and the years turned in to decades, the story of Tara Calico was shown to a National audience on several other venues including *48 hours* and *America's Most Wanted*. With all of the exposure came an influx of tips and leads for investigators to sort through. The case of the disappearance of Tara Calico remained unsolved with no credible leads. The investigation was entirely cold.

It was not until 2008, nearly 20 years since Tara had disappeared, that this case would return to the fore front of the media. Valencia County, New Mexico Sheriff Renee Rivera released a statement claiming that he knew exactly what had happened to Tara. The problem, however, that he indicated is that the body of Tara Calico had never been found. This would make it impossible to bring those responsible, or at least who he felt was responsible, to justice.

"The individuals who did harm to Tara knew who she was. They knew who she was, and they are all local individuals. And I believe that the parents of the attackers were some of the people that helped the individuals with hiding the truth or hiding the body or trying to escape persecution," Rivera said.

Rivera never gave the suspects names. Rivera did, however, give his belief on what happened to Tara. Sheriff Rivera claims that two teenagers, roughly the same age as Tara, were involved in the crime. He also believed that several of the men's family members helped to cover up the crime.

"You know it's very frustrating, being that there's a lot of people who know what happened," Rivera said. "They know the whereabouts of the body or the remains. I believe that the body is somewhere very close. The body is somewhere very nearby."

Rivera had been approached by many informants over the previous couple of years. The informants all shared similar stories to what really happened to Tara Calico. According to the informants and Renee Rivera's statements, Tara never made it more than a few miles from her house on September 20, 1989. She was struck by the two teenagers who were driving a pickup truck. Rather than alert authorities and handle the situation the right way, the boys told their families and the families helped to bury the body of Tara Calico. The informants attest that the intention was not to hit Tara Calico, but to approach her while she was on her bike.

"She was really pretty young girl. She was very athletic, and a lot of guys wanted to talk to her, they wanted to meet her, they wanted to go out with her. And while she was riding her bike, they went up to try to talk to her, try to grab her, whatever, while she was on the bike," Rivera said.

Many people have questioned the basis of Sheriff Rivera's claims. While the claims do make sense and would line up with the evidence that investigators had uncovered, why is it 20 years later that the Sheriff would come out and voice these claims. If Rivera had such strong reason to make these allegations and had informants that were willing to speak as to what happened, why has there been no conviction? This is a question that remains to be answered.

Sadly, in 2006, Patty Doel, the mother of Tara Calico, passed away. She dealt with such a heavy heart and severe burden since Tara's disappearance in 1989. She passed away never knowing the truth as to what happened to Tara on the fateful day. Tara's father passed away in 2002 as well. Tara Calico's family never recovered from that dreadful morning, and never got the answers they needed for any sort of effort of closure. Tara's family is still searching for the truth of the events of that day. Thanks to social media, there are thousands of people nationwide that have joined in to find any answers or leads that may result in the truth.

The identity of the boy in the photograph still remains a mystery as well. The fact that neither victim in the photograph has ever been fully confirmed or identified remains a great mystery. While most every investigator will attest that woman in the photograph is indeed Tara Calico, there is no way to match an identity without the actual DNA evidence.

The story of Tara Calico is undeniably tragic. The truth is largely unknown. There have been no arrest and no attempts at arrest in the years since the horrific disappearance. While many believe the overall story that Sheriff Rivera told as to what had really happened to Tara, there has been no attempts to convict anyone of the heinous crime. The only true fact of this case is that a promising future was cut short while she was enjoying a beautiful September day. Perhaps one day the mystery of Tara Calico will be fully understood. Perhaps one day justice will come forth and healing can begin.

THE DISAPPEARANCE OF APRIL PITZER

LARRY MARAVICH

The Mojave Desert is a place of extremes. Burning days and freezing nights. Promises of hope, tales of despair. Home to the gold rush, littered with iron deposits and arrays of silver and tungsten, its extensive salt deposits give rise to borax and potash. To the south, and into Mexico lies the hotter Sonoran Desert, while the Mojave itself extends to a huge, empty 25000 square miles. It reaches into Nevada, Arizona, Utah and California.

Communities are few and far between, and it is a land of wanderers, of hermits, of people finding their way in life – or finding themselves increasingly lost, mentally as well as geographically. The land is as much of a roller coaster as the emotional journey many of its inhabitants face; the Mojave contains the hottest place in the US – Death Valley – and the lowest (near Badwater).

The region itself seems full of unhealed wounds – the ground is pitted with mines, mostly abandoned. It is in one of these that, it is believed, the body of a young, beautiful woman now rests.

The disappearance of April Pitzer, missing for so long that she has been officially declared as being dead, is an especially tragic story. It is a tale of girl who makes one bad decision. From that a promising life ends in death and an eternity to be endured most probably deep down a mine shaft. The body as abandoned as the pothole in which it lies. This story co-stars a mother who will not give up hope that her daughter's body might someday be found.

April was only three years old when she was taken from her home and put into the care of relatives. Gloria Denton was nineteen at the time and judged not able to look after her young daughter. But despite this, the two stayed close, sharing letters and cards. April grew up a smiling, cheery girl, one whose features moved from childish charm to outright beauty.

She would, for a time, work as a model. It was when she was seventeen, and able to make the decision for herself as to who would be responsible for her well-being, that she made the call to move back in with her mother. The two became best friends – the age gap was not great, and many described the relationship between the couple as more sisterly than that of a mother and daughter. April and Gloria developed a bond that had been denied to them first separated.

For a while, all seemed great. But early trauma leaves its impact. – and being taken from your mother, even if looked after by loving relatives, can only be described as a trauma. The mind is pitted, scarred like the remnants left behind by a cyst. When April fell in with a bad crowd, one that dabbled in drugs, took on too much alcohol, it was not especially different to the experiences many young men and women have. One day, April went a little too far, and was caught driving under the influence of alcohol.

Although a relatively minor crime, police saw an opportunity to use her arrest as a lever to open up bigger crimes. They put the proposition to April that her misdemeanour would be let go if she agreed to appear as a witness in a drugs' case. That particular investigation was in its early stages and would not come to fruition for many years. Without the benefit of experience in such matters and seeing a short-term solution to a problem she had created, April leapt at the chance. What the young model did not know was that the DEA were finding evidence of an enormous drugs ring, making and distributing amphetamines, and that she held information on some of the participants.

But that investigation would take six years to come to fruition. In the meantime, April moved on with her life. All was happy, and in 2000 she married Chase Pitzer. Things started well and her mother reported how much the two were in love. When their first child came along, a daughter, it seemed as though life was perfect.

But her promise to act as a witness for the DEA was about to come back and haunt April. It was about to change her life forever. She was living quietly in Fort Worth, Texas when there was a knock on the door.

It was the DEA. They had arrived to take April back to Arkansas, to act as a witness in a trial involving people from a life she had left behind.

Ultimately, over thirty people were convicted. April changed. Her mother pinpoints the alteration in her daughter to the end of that trial. April became convinced that friends and relatives of the people she had helped to get incarcerated were out to get her, that they would hunt her down and hurt her. Even more frightening, that they might hurt her daughter. The problems with paranoia are that it is real to the sufferer, and hard to understand for others. Chase felt that she had nothing to worry about, she was living in a different state, and would be hard to find, even if there was a desire on anybody's part to do this, which there probably was not.

But April could not see beyond the fear, the looking over her shoulder, the shadows in her mind. Even the birth of their second daughter provided only a brief period of happiness. The respite from her worries were short lived. The inevitable happened, Chase and April grew apart. Her mother does not blame her ex son in law. She recognises that her daughter was the one with the problem. But like any mother, she wanted to protect her daughter. It was not possible to do so. Depression followed, along with a return to drink and drugs. Medication was prescribed, and April started to become dependent on the alien products she was pushing into her body.

Then, with a frightening parallel, history repeated herself. Just as Gloria had been separated from the ones she loved, so was April. Her daughters were placed into the care of her in laws, the grounds given being that April was now suffering from a bi-polar disorder and was not capable of looking after her girls properly. The nightmare of separation she had suffered herself as a small child was about happen again.

April was not a well woman. Her marriage was destroyed, her children taken, her life a mixture of periods of desire to do whatever it took to get her children back, punctuated by moments of simply not being able to cope.

In her disturbed state she made the decision to head west, into the heart of the Mojave Desert. In that mysterious, mystical landscape the belief that life would improve was strong. April became convinced that if she removed herself from the scene, her in laws would realise that they needed her to look after her children, that they would not be able to cope without her. 'Distance makes the heart grow fonder,' she told her mother.

In the desert, she met up with a truck driver, John Lopez. The attraction was immediate, and John was happy to offer her the love, attention and time that she craved at this low point in her life. Gloria is convinced that the relationship had a dual purpose for her daughter. Yes, she was grateful to John Lopez, and welcomed the attention he was able to give. But there was an ulterior motive in her daughter's plans. She believes, to this day, that the main reason for April's brief time with John lay in the deepest corners of her confused mind. That Chase would come running to reclaim his true love, that his family would crave her return to look after their children. It was the delusion of a sad young lady suffering from mental ill health.

It seems as though her upbringing, away from her mother, had planted the seeds of this condition, and the fear that followed acting as a witness against the drugs cartel had watered them until they flourished inside April's head, causing her to behave in a way that was irrational.

Because, underneath it all, she remained a caring, loving woman. Soon, she would be giving her time to help an ill old woman. Some people say that we are all nurses or patients. April needed to be the latter, but tried to be the former.

The situation above arose from the following convoluted course. One day, she was attending a party outside of Barstow, California. This desert town possessed a much unwanted reputation. It was known as the drugs capital of the Mojave. Downbeat, and within the borders of the desert, the town contained areas to avoid and people with whom it was best to steer clear.

John Lopez had warned April of this, had tried to ease her towards the safer parts. But that relationship had been built on the shifting sands of the Mojave and was already struggling. The party featured alcohol and drugs in extreme. There she met a man who offered her a home in one of his trailers, which she gladly accepted, leaving immediately on his motorbike. In fact, the trailer was a wreck, isolated and without basic services. The people living in the surrounding park, if such a word can be used to describe the boulder strewn, barren area, are not ones with which she wants to spend her life. In despair, and with nothing, she sets off along the deserted desert highway heading for wherever. A kindly truck driver sees her, stops to check she is OK, and seeing her despair takes her to see his aging and ill mother.

Barbara Killebrew and April Pitzer hit it off straight away. Maybe Barbara provided the mother figure, or more likely grandmotherly presence, April never had – her relationship with her real mother, remember, was immensely close, but at that time more sisterly than that of a mother and her child. Perhaps Barbara provided April with the opportunity to express the love and care she needed to give to somebody, with her own daughters unable to receive that giving.

Whatever the case, April was a regular visitor, enjoying the time she spent caring for and talking with Barbara. She would have lived there but the small home had no spare bedroom. Instead, April relied on the friends she had begun to establish during her time with John Lopez. One of those was Steve Wilkinson. Himself a former inmate for drugs related crime, he was now on the straight and narrow, but knew the community in that part of California. Steve was aware of who it was safe to mix with, and who not. For a very brief period it seemed to April that things were looking up. She had a friend in Barbara whom she could trust. A friend in Steve who offered some protection.

Then, she saw a face from the past. A woman whom she recognised as the wife of a man she had helped to put away. The paranoia, the fear, swept back into her life. Having been on the verge of returning home to her mother, once again she dreaded what might happen.

Steve tried to reassure her. He had spoken to the woman, and she had no wish to pursue the past. What had happened had happened, the woman told Steve, and it was over now. But April could not be persuaded. She rang her mother who, not used to the world in which her daughter had found herself, and upset by April's panic, gave what was perhaps not the advice she needed to hear.

'You gotta get out of there...' Gloria blurted 'You're gonna die.'

April said she knew of a place where she would be safe. Chuck Hollister – Uncle Chuck – took people down on their luck into his house, located in nearby Newberry Springs. From there, she could still see Barbara, but would also be safe. She begged her mother to send some clothing, to help her cope in her penniless state with the freezing Mojave nights, and promised that she would be home soon.

Gloria packed clothes immediately and awaited her daughter's return. She was convinced that April was ready to come home. Later, detectives would question this, sensing that it was a mother persuading herself to believe what she wanted to believe. In any case, April did not immediately head for home. But she began to get ready to do so.

She borrowed some cases from Barbara, who needed to spend some time in hospital to receive closer, expert care for a while. She packed the clothes her mother had sent. She prepared to go home, paying for the bus ride with the money her mother had sent her. April was 30, and needed to head back to mom and, she hoped, soon reunite with her children. Maybe even Chase as well.

Chuck Hollister was on a business trip the day April planned to head back to Arkansas. Some reports say he left her sleeping in bed, others that he dropped her at the bus station. Gloria waited for daughter to show up. And waited. And waited.

As hours turned into days she tried to ring April. But her daughter had no cell phone – she could not afford one – and Chuck was not answering. The days turned into weeks and Gloria tried to report her daughter missing. She had been due home on June 28th and had not appeared. The local police were not interested. April was a mature woman. One who was suffering from bi-polar disorder, whose marriage had broken up and who was missing her children. She was not a priority case, and had most probably simply taken a walk, a trip elsewhere into the vast, empty expanse of the Mojave Desert.

But Gloria knew differently. Mothers do. It was July 16th 2004 that Gloria unsuccessfully tried to report her daughter as missing, but three days later she received a phone call from Chuck Hollister. He had been away, he said. He had taken April to collect her stuff from Barbara's home on a couple of days previously and had expected April to be gone on his return from his trip – she had told him how much she was missing her children and could not wait to see them.

Then, on his return, her suitcase was there. She had just decided, he thought, to spend longer in the desert. Probably, she had gone wandering once more. A few days later, Barbara too got in touch, to see how April was doing, to wish her well and to thank for her the support she had given.

Now Gloria had proof that her daughter was missing. April had told Barbara that she was leaving to return home. She had not made it. The police were finally prepared to listen and distributed missing person posters all around the area. The first, small, breakthrough came on September fourth. A local bus driver reported that a passenger had seen one of the missing person posters.

'I know where she's at,' claimed the witness 'she's in a hole.'

Police traced the witness, who they did not name, but she changed her story. This time, she said that she did not know exactly where April was. However, at a party another person had said to her that April had been killed and thrown down a mineshaft. It looked as though a murder investigation was about to be launched.

But the Deputy Coroner, David Van Norman, put matters into perspective. There were no less than twenty thousand mine shafts in St Bernardino County alone; let alone the entirety of the Mojave Desert. Trying to pinpoint one that held April Pitzer would be an impossible task. Harder than tracing a needle in a haystack, he said. It was not just the case that there were so many mine shafts. Many were extremely deep, with virtually vertical passages in places. The state of repair of the majority was so poor as to make them highly dangerous to enter. Most had not been explored for a hundred years or more. Rock falls would have occurred, and pit props would rot in the humid underground conditions. Some were only yards long, others might interlock with neighbouring mines, running off into passages and offshoots.

Without more information, the chances of locating a body – one that might not even be there – were extremely remote. Then, a little while later, a bizarre clue – the first of several – set police off hunting in a smaller area. Eight hundred miles away a piece of graffiti hinted that someone might know a little more.

'Looking for missing girl from Arkansas,' it read, scrawled on the walls of a truck stop two day's driving distant. 'Three Miles Barstow, 1-15 Freeway.'

Was it a joke? Was it something deliberately sent to mislead police? They could not know for sure, but if there was any value in the message, it was still limited. Within three miles of Barstow there were hundreds of mine shafts. Not the tens of thousands that existed in the desert as a whole, but still far too many for anything like a search.

Instead, police scanned CCTV coverage of the area, looking back from the end of June of that year onwards. It was a long, onerous task – many tapes were recorded over, and after the many man hours of scrutiny the police had discovered...nothing.

Meanwhile, Gloria was contacting as many of April's friends and associates from the area as she could. With no phone of her own, April had relied on borrowing those of her friends to contact her mother. But although snippets of information came forward, mostly they were stabs in the dark, unsubstantiated theories and rumour. The investigation was going nowhere. But among the numerous suggestions, one thing came up more than any other.

The mines around Ludlow. A friend of Chuck Hollister, who called himself 'Dan Dan' (proper name, Dan Dansbury), lived close by, and claimed to own a mine there, one that went by the name of Red Dog Mine. Dan Dan was a man with a reputation. Whether it was one based on reality, or the constructs of a mind living out a fantasy, nobody was sure. Certainly, he claimed to have been a sniper in Vietnam, but there was no evidence to back up the assertion.

Steve Wilkinson, the friend with whom April had lodged, knew Dan Dan from way back, when he had been a younger and feared member of the neighbourhood. 'One of the guys you didn't want to cross.'

Hand written signs littered Red Dog Cave, some of them barely literate.

'You can leave, or you can disapear (sic). I can help you to disapear no problem' read one. Another stated. 'Three people can keep a secret if two of them are dead.' Detective Steve Pennington was a police officer working the case, and he felt that it was worth speaking to Dan Dan. That proved hard to do. Dan Dan spent a lot of time with Chuck Hollister, the two enjoyed exploring the caves. Dan Dan often spent days at a time living in Red Dog Mine, he would search for rocks and gems from which to make jewellery and such like, always hoping that a rich vein of untapped gold or other minerals would be found. Judging from the state of his rotting home, he was never lucky.

Pennington would arrive at the home, but even if the hermit's truck was there, the door would not be answered. However, finally, contact was made, but Dan Dan denied any knowledge about the disappearance of April. Nevertheless, police felt that here was something that they could at least investigate. The brought in cadaver dogs, canines trained to find the bodies of the dead. The dogs were lowered on harnesses and spent two days searching for a clue. Nothing was found. Another dead end.

In January 2005 another clue emerged. The owner of a well-known local eatery, The Bagdad Café in Newberry Springs, saw one of the missing posters and thought that she knew the subject. Andrea Pruett contacted police. April had walked into the café one day last summer asking about work. Pruett was reluctant; the girl looked grubby and business was slow. But keen to give a person a chance, she offered some temporary work as a waitress. When April showed up to begin her new job, she was transformed – on day one at least. She was smartly dressed in white and black, tidy with her hair up. She was friendly with customers, and Pruett thought that she had discovered a gem. But on day two, April was transformed. Her face bore evidence of a beating, and she seemed withdrawn. Although she tried to chat to her new employee, Pruett found herself questioning a brick wall.

Day three never happened, April did not turn up again. That was June 28th 2004. Maybe that was the day April disappeared. Nothing more was found on the case for nearly a year. A year of complete hell for Gloria. Her daughter had been taken from her once, and now it was happening again.

Assistant Coroner David Van Norman called the Desert Historian, somebody who knew the mines better than anybody. He asked for a special look out to be kept.

Then, in December 2005 Norman's wisdom garnered a result. Out on a guided tour of the mines, the Historian took a group into a cavern he rarely visited. There, he stumbled on some clothes. Calling the group away, he contacted the investigators as soon as it was possible to do so. Gloria caught the first plane out, and made her way to the

Indian Queen Mine, where the discovery had been made. For the first time, she saw the barren expanse of void for what it was. She recalled two things that April had said to her in their phone calls, before she disappeared. 'It's a dog eat dog world,' and 'You do what you can to survive.'. Under the beating heat, looking at the abandoned mine, seeing the dead lands, overlooked by far off bleak and barren mountains, she knew exactly what her daughter meant.

But as for the clothes, they were definitely her daughter's. Gloria recognised a checked flannel shirt she had sent out to protect against the cold nights. It was a devastating moment; surely the shirt was evidence that April was, indeed, dead. She might have heard the rumours and half stories of third hand witnesses, but now she had something concrete in her hands.

From there, she persuaded police to go back to Red Dog Mine, convinced that Dan Dan, and possibly Hollister, were involved. If they were not directly responsible for the crime, she believed that they knew more about it. At the mine, police made an astonishing discovery. They found one of the suitcases Barbara Killebrow had leant to her friend. Clothing was scattered over a three-mile radius. Police were sure that the case had not been there when they first searched the area around the mine. They widened their search, with renewed hope, and other discoveries came to light. A nightgown Gloria insisted had belonged to her daughter was found twisted into the shape of a noose in a barn twelve miles away. In that shack were strips of cloth and iodine. A third series of searches took place in Red Dog Mine, and this time discoveries were made. An old mattress, hidden deep inside and stained with bodily fluids. Undergarments, boots and other clothes.

Had Hollister taken the case to the mine in a fit of bizarre behaviour? Did Dan Dansbury know more than he was letting on? The two became suspects but denied any involvement in April's disappearance. Hollister was also seriously ill. He had terminal cancer and died in September 2006. To Gloria, he and Dan Dan were the obvious prime suspects, but nothing could be proved.

Then, in 2009, a double bend of a change in the direction of the case took place. Gloria received a call from Dan Dan begging that she come to see him. Expecting a difficult, bitter meeting she went. There, she found Dan close to death. He spoke in glowing terms of April, said that he had known her and that she had been a wonderful person. The two cried together. Gloria's view of Dan changed. No longer could she see him as a cold-blooded killer. Indeed, her suspicions flew back to her first theory, that April had been found by an associate of one of the drug dealers she had helped to put away.

But, in one of his final communications before death claimed him, Dan is alleged to have shifted position again and left one more clue. He is said to have told a friend: 'They are looking in the right place. Just not far enough.' Did he know more about the real resting place of April Pitzer? Was he covering for his friend, Chuck Hollister? Did he himself have some sort of role in the former model's death? Or, was this just a return to the fantasy world in which he seemed to live, one that cast him as Vietnam hero and one of society's outcasts, on the brink of the sort of find in his mine that would make his fortune?

In 2010, a further attempt was made to search for April's body. Local mining experts, with access to advanced equipment, supported Steve Pennington and the police by searching once more the caves in the Ludlow area. These included the Red Dog Mine, the Indian Queen and others in the nearby Elephant Mountain complex.

They found more clothing, tattered now but according to Gloria definitely belonging to her daughter. Gloria said that April liked to cut a V shape in the labels on her clothes, and that alteration was found in the recovered shirts. The discovery was made within fifteen feet of the surface of a disused mine, one whose entrance was partially hidden. Whether that was the result of natural rockfall, or an attempt to cover tracks, it was impossible to say.

But once more, despite extensive searches far underground, nothing definitive was discovered.

For a short while, Steve Wilkinson too came into the frame. But the long haired, hippyish looking former drug manufacturer denied any involvement. The only evidence linking him to the crime was a report that he had been spied near the Red Dog Mine around the time of her disappearance. But, Wilkinson was a friend of Chuck Hollister, an associate of Dan Dan. There are many completely innocent reasons why he could have been in that vicinity, if indeed he was. And like the other named suspects, he too is now dead, killed when the light aircraft in which he was travelling crashed into a Colorado mountain.

And so, April Pitzer most probably lies somewhere under the Mojave Desert, the victim of an attack - perhaps carried out by someone she knew, maybe the victim of an organised drugs gang. Perhaps even she died as the victim of a random assault. She was declared officially dead in August 2012, and her mother no longer believes that she is buried in a disused Californian mine, although she thinks that this may once have been true.

But we can be assured that Gloria Denton will not stop searching for news of her missing daughter until her body is found, or she too passes on to another life.

SEARCHING FOR MAURA MURRAY

ANDREA TORRENCE

The case of Maura Murray's disappearance is one that has left police and conspiracy theorists baffled for more than a decade. Her sudden disappearance is one that makes very little sense and the available information regarding who she is as a person and her motive behind her attempt to leave town prior to vanishing isn't easy to wrap our brains around.

Maura has been missing since February 9, 2004. From the time of her disappearance, there have been no credible sightings of Maura. The last person to see her alive, a passing motorist, noticed her oddly calm demeanor following a car crash, but she was gone by the time the police arrived on the scene.

Her family is devastated that they haven't gotten closure, but is also skeptical that she could still be alive. Laurie and Fred, Maura's mother and father, have had nothing to add regarding their daughter's disappearance, and have no idea what thought pushed her into taking some personal belongings, withdrawing over $200 in cash, and attempting to leave town under the guise of "grieving over a death in the family."

To get an understanding of the case, it's important to understand who Maura is, what she did and said in the days prior to her disappearance, and her strange behavior moments before vanishing into thin air.

Maura was born on May 4, 1982, in Hanson, Massachusetts. She is the third child of four (two older sisters, one younger brother) and had a normal upbringing as a child. Her parents divorced when she was 6 years old and she mainly stayed with her mother. She was a very athletic person during her high school years at Whitman-Hanson Regional High. After graduating from high school, she was accepted into the United States Military Academy in New York, where she took chemical engineering for three semesters. However, after her freshmen year at the academy, she was under threat of disciplinary action and expulsion.

This prompted her to transfer to the University of Massachusetts Amherst.

For Maura, her sophomore and junior years at UMass were pretty much uneventful, except for her meeting with boyfriend and future-fiancé Bill Rausch. She was doing well academically and attracted very little attention for the wrong people.

To most people, Maura Murray was living the normal college school-girl life: lots of friends, getting good grades, going to parties, and even holding a steady job at her college. Her father told reporters that Maura was on the dean's list, a list of high-achieving students who receive recognition for their college's dean. Rausch's mother, Sharon Rausch, spoke of being ecstatic at the news of her daughter's engagement to her boyfriend and they were understandingly busy planning the wedding.

However, in November 2003, three months before her disappearance, things turned sour in Maura's life as she admitted to using stolen credit cards to order food. However, her case was continued the following month, and was to be dismissed if she showed three months of good behavior. Unfortunately, she never got the chance to meet the three-month deadline.

Maura's life turned from sour to extremely strange when on the evening of February 5, 2004, she was having a phone conversation with Kathleen, one of her old sisters, while on duty at her security guard job at her college. It was reported that the sisters mainly talked about their respective fiancés and whatever problems they were having. Something about the phone call made Maura appear physically upset and at around 10:30 PM she finally broke down in tears. When her supervisor went to see her at her desk, she appeared "just completely zoned out. No reaction at all. She was unresponsive."

At around 1:30 AM on February 6, 2004, her supervisor ended her shift early and brought her back to her dorms. Her supervisor asked her what was wrong, but Maura seemed reluctant to answer. Finally she told her supervisor, "My sister." Assuming the worst and not wanting to intrude on personal matters, her boss had no further line of questioning and left her at her dorm.

Only recently were the contents of the phone conversation between Maura and Kathleen disclosed to the public. Kathleen told reporters that they both talked of Kathleen recovering from her alcoholism. After being discharged from a rehabilitation clinic that evening the phone call was made, her fiancé took her directly to a liquor store. Kathleen recalled being upset that he was less understanding of her rocky situation, but soon become intoxicated along with him. This caused an emotional breakdown for Kathleen, and after telling her younger sister about it, Maura too seemed on the verge of breaking down herself. Before this information was disclosed, rumors speculated that Maura's answer to her supervisor ("My sister") was just a random string of words with little meaning, and in fact had more of a general family crisis.

On February 7, 2004, Fred Murray came to visit his daughter at Amherst, Massachusetts. His intention of coming to see his third daughter was to take her car-shopping that afternoon and have dinner together. After dining together, Maura took her father back to the motel where he was staying, and got permission to take her father's car back to her university where she was supposed to attend a party. She took the Toyota Corolla and arrived at her dorms at 10:30 PM.

At 2:30 AM on February 8th, she left the party and started the trip back to her father's motel where she was planning on spending the night. However, at 3:30 AM, en route to the motel, she struck a guardrail, causing almost $10,000 worth of damages to the car. The police were alerted of the accident and the responding officer filled and filed the accident report, but did not include any documentation regarding carrying out a field sobriety test on Maura. The officer took her to her father's motel where she would remain until that afternoon.

That morning, Fred Murray discovered that the damages to his vehicle would be covered by his car insurance, so he rented a car and dropped Maura off at her college before making the trip to Connecticut. That night at 11:30 PM, he called Maura to remind her to get the accident report forms from the Registry of Motor Vehicles. They made plans to talk again via telephone the next day where he would instruct her on how to fill out the insurance claim form.

On Monday, February 9, 2004, the available information of Maura's actions seemed out of character for the 21-year old nursing student. At around noon, using her PC, Maura searched MapQuest – a free mapping service available online – to look for directions to the Berkshires and Burlington, Vermont. It remains unclear why Maura looked up direction to the Berkshires, but she did make reservations at a hotel in Burlington.

At 1:00 PM that day, she made her contact with another person, her boyfriend, through email. In her email she wrote:

"I love you more stud. I got your messages, but honestly, I didn't feel like talking to [sic] *much to anyone, I promise to call today though."*

It is also unclear what she messages she received and how Rausch sent messages to Maura. Her next conversation with another person was with a condominium owner in Bartlett, New Hampshire – the same condo association her family would frequently visit in the past. From her telephone records, we see that the phone conversation lasted around three minutes, and the owner ultimately did not end up renting out a condominium to Maura. After this, Maura called a classmate at her college, but the contents of their conversation are unknown.

At 1:24 PM, Maura emailed her work supervisor at the college and requested a full week of leave due to a supposed "death in the family." Subsequent reports from her family found that her reasoning was falsified as there were no known deaths in either her mother or father's respective families at the time. Maura promised to make contact with her supervisor by the time she got back. Remembering her uncontrollable sobbing several nights before, her supervisor granted her request for a one-week leave.

Maura's phone records also show that she made contact with a hotel in Stowe, Vermont, regarding reservations of a hotel room. This is the second reservation she made that night after the one for a room in Burlington, Vermont. This phone call lasted around five minutes, and at 2:18 PM she called her boyfriend but reached his voicemail. She left a message, promising that they would speak again. This call lasted about one minute, and that was the last phone call she made that day.

Before taking off to wherever she wanted to go, she prepared for her trip by packing some clothes, toiletries, college books, and birth-control pills. Classes that day were cancelled following a snowstorm that struck the city, so at approximately 3:30 PM Maura made her way off campus in her black Saturn. After the police searched her room, they found that most of her personal belongings were stored in boxes and all of her art pieces were taken down from the walls. It's unknown whether Maura packed the items that day, but police concluded that it was done between Sunday night and Monday morning. Maura left a printed message on top of the boxes which addressed her boyfriend and indicated troubles they were having in their relationship.

At 3:40 PM, her bank records show that Maura withdrew $280 for her account at an ATM, and CCTV shows that she entered and left the ATM alone. She made her way to a liquor store located nearby and purchased roughly $40 worth of alcoholic drinks. Visual records of the transaction also show that Maura was alone at the time of her purchase. She subsequently made her way to the Massachusetts Registry of Motor Vehicles and picked up the accident report forms as per her father's request.

She then left Amherst – most likely through Interstate 91 north – and called her voicemail at 4:37 PM to check for messages. This was the last recorded instance where Maura is known to have used her cell phone. It is believed that she did not tell her travel plans to anybody and she did not let anyone know where she was headed. Even her father whom she had had a loving relationship with was unaware of where her daughter would go.

"In my position as father," Fred Murray begins, *"you would think that maybe there would be something said... But I had no hint. I thought everything was okay. I wasn't aware of any stuff like school problems. She was on the dean's list in a very difficult program [nursing program]."*

Around 7:00 PM on February 9, 2004, a woman from Woodsville, New Hampshire, heard a loud noise from outside her home. Peering from her window, she saw a sedan resting alongside a snow bank on Route 112. She immediately notified the Grafton County Sheriff's Department at 7:27 PM. From the 911 log, the woman mentioned seeing a man with a lit cigarette inside of the car, but later changed her statement that she had neither seen a man nor a cigarette but instead she saw a red glow, possibly from an active cell phone.

One of the woman's neighbors, a school bus driver headed home from work, saw a woman inside of the car who appeared to be uninjured but freezing from the cold. He offered to call for help on the woman's behalf but she pleaded for him to not alert the police of her situation. She went on to say that she called AAA and they were already headed her way, but subsequent reports found that Maura never contacted AAA. The school bus driver was aware that that particular area had no telecommunications signal but didn't push the issue. He went home and called reported what he witnessed to the local authorities.

The man made the call at 7:47 PM but was not in view of the sedan so he didn't know when the police had arrived, but he did notice that several other cars pass from the direction of the sedan. Another local from Woodsville claimed to have seen a police SUV parked directly in front of the SUV at 7:37 PM, saw that nobody was in or around the cars and promptly headed back home. However, this report contradicted the official police records which show that the Haverhill police arrived at the scene of the accident 9 minutes later.

The police records state that the first officer to arrive at the scene appeared at 7:46 PM. No person was found in or around the vehicle which was physically damaged. Later inspections found that the collision had knocked the car's radiator into the fan, completely ruining the car's heating system. Both airbags were deployed the windshield was cracked on the driver's side. The car was locked when the officer arrived, but he reported seeing red stains around the interior of the car, possibly from red wine. He also found an empty bottle of beer and a box of Franzia wine on the rear seats.

Other contents of the car included an accident report form, CDs, makeup, diamond jewelry, an AAA card belonging to Maura Murray, two sets of MapQuest directions for Burlington and Stowe, Vermont), a stuffed animal later identified as Maura's favorite doll, and a mountain-climbing book set in the White Mountains. No trace of a debit card, credit card, or cell phone was found and there are no records showing that they have been used ever since her disappearance.

The responding office went on the search for Maura with the help of the school bus driver. They were searching for Maura in the surrounding area of the crash site before an ambulance and a fire truck arrived. At 8:49 PM, the sedan was towed to a local garage, and a rag was found stuffed inside of the car's tailpipe. The rag is believed to be a part of Maura's emergency roadside kit. About 24 hours after the incident and unable to locate Maura, she officially became a "missing" person.

Sharon Rausch spoke of how Maura had a history of car troubles, possibly due to her own bad driving. Sharon told reporters, *"I knew she was having car trouble. We had gotten her a AAA membership with the long-distance towing because we were concerned about her."*

The frantic search for Maura began at 12:36 PM the day following her disappearance. A "Be on the lookout" report was released, reporting her possible last outfit and accessories she brought with her.

On February 11th, after being informed of his daughter's sudden disappearance and her abandoned car 140 miles away from her dorm room, Fred Murray makes the night-long drive from his job at Bridgeport, Connecticut. *"I get [to New Hampshire] at daybreak to join the search."* Her mother Laurie has to sit and wait at her home in Hanson, Massachusetts, for updates of her missing daughter due to an ankle injury.

Eventually the family along with boyfriend Bill Rausch and his mother and father join the search in New Hampshire for the missing woman. However, en route to New Hampshire from Fort Sill, Oklahoma, Bill Rausch received a voice message from an unknown person. He told his mother about the phone call and was absolutely sure that the call came from his girlfriend. He publicized the contents of the message to reporters not long after the search for Maura began. *"The message basically, in and of itself, was just a woman breathing and possibly a whimper or some sort of noise at the end which we believed to be her."*

The mysterious voice message that Bill received could quite possibly be from his missing girlfriend, but there is no explanation as to how Maura got hold of another person's cell phone. Her own phone hasn't been in use since the afternoon of February 5th. Bill tried calling the phone back but it was a prepaid calling card and the number was unreachable.

At 5:00 PM on February 11, 2004, a police K9 picked up Maura's scent and located one of her gloves 100 yards away from where her damaged vehicle was found, but lost the scent afterwards. This suggested to the police that Maura may have possibly gotten into another vehicle and left the area. Upon his arrival, Bill Rausch was interrogated by police in private then soon joined by both of his parents. At 7:00 PM the police believed that Murray may have come to Woodsville, New Hampshire, to either escape her life or commit suicide, two theories that her family outright rejected.

One of the only credible sightings of Maura after her disappearance came from a contractor who was on his way home from Franconia, New Hampshire. From between 8:00 and 8:30 PM, he claims to have witnessed a young person walking quickly on Route 112 – a location roughly 5 miles away from Maura's initial crash site and where her car was found. He described the late-night walker to be sporting a dark coat, jeans, and a bright-colored hood. The contractor initially didn't report anything to the police, but 3 months later found out that the walker may have been Maura Murray who disappeared the same day he saw the mysterious, hooded person.

What made the story of Maura Murray's disappearance become nation- and even world-wide news is the fact that it happened during the social media age. In mid 2000s, people were accustomed to seeing fake news floating freely throughout the internet, and at first Maura's case was dismissed as uninteresting and even made up. However, as the media dug deeper and uncovered basically nothing regarding Maura's speculated whereabouts or where she was heading, her missing case was swiftly picked up by a number of independent website creators. In 2005, Maura's story was picked up and documented by websleuths.com – an internet community focused mainly on missing persons and crime – and by 2007, Facebook and MySpace pages dedicated to locating the missing woman were launched. It appeared as if all of the country was looking for the nursing student from UMass Amherst.

Fred Murray has repeatedly returned to the scene of the accident in order to do his own personal searching for his beloved daughter. He made mention of how Maura was unfamiliar with the area past Route 112. The roads at nighttime are a hazard to drivers who aren't familiar with the path. For the days, months and years after his daughter's disappearance, he still remains hopeful for answers despite the lack of leads and suspects. Fred said, *"It was just like yesterday to me. I guess it always will be until I find out what happened."* Sharon Rauch has commented on Fred's dedication to his daughter, *"God has just blessed him and given him the strength. He goes up there week after week and he keeps searching the sides of the roads, he keeps searching the woods."*

Serious allegations against Bill Rausch, Maura's ex-boyfriend and now a married father, have surfaced in the recent past. Three women have voiced their accusations against Rausch (two through radio interviews, the third with private talks with the police) and have linked him to the disappearance of Maura in 2004. Bill has an alibi for the evening of his then-girlfriend's vanishing (he was at Fort Sill, Oklahoma, at the time) but rumors speak of there being a tandem driver who picked and dropped Maura off before the police could find her. Whether the tandem driver was an accessory to a conspiracy conspired by Rausch, there's probably no way to tell. In the end, we all have to understand that Bill Rausch, no matter how sketchy his history with women is, has never been a potential suspect in Maura's case.

Maura's family reflects back at the choices made by their missing daughter during the days before her sudden disappearance. *"I don't know why she came to New Hampshire,"* Fred Murray says, *"I don't know. I'd be guessing the same as everybody else."* Sadly, there is no conclusion to the story of the missing 21-year old aspiring nurse. Nowadays, it appears as if the case has gone cold, and it has been many a year since she any new information has surfaced.

In November 2017, the internet exploded when there was news that the New Hampshire Police Department was going to officially reopen the case of Maura Murray after several years or silence. The announcement came after Oxygen aired the season finale of their documentary investigation, *The Disappearance of Maura Murray*, which reviewed the case from beginning to end. Journalist and UMass alum Maggie Freleng worked together with a retired US Marshal and the Murray family in an attempt to put a nail on the 13-year old case's coffin. The ex-Marshal reported in the series that the department was going to take another look at "all the forensics, re-examining everything from day one."

However, it turns out that only weeks after the case was going to be "reopened," Oxygen retracted their statement since the department never officially closed the case to begin with. Jeffrey Strelzin, the Chief of the Homicide Unit in the New Hampshire Attorney General's Office, told reporters that he saw bits of the investigative series of the Murray case and found many inconsistencies with reality. He further added that the whole series in general is not to be considered an investigative one since its parallelism with the truth is, at times, nonexistent.

Despite the series failure to be in line with the realities of the Missing Murray case, it shows how much the present-day society has taken an interest in Maura as a person and as a citizen of the country. Not many missing people have been able to garner as much interest as Maura has, and this just makes the whole case much more urgent to find closure.

Throughout the last 13 years, every so often we see new news articles and videos regarding the Maura's absence, but her family is still hopeful that she'll reappear. There's no losing hope with Fred Murray who has dedicated his time and efforts in bringing awareness to the problem in search of providing closure. There's nothing more important than finally putting the case of their beloved daughter to rest.

It's difficult to put our feet into Fred's shoes as he has been living in his own personal hell for the last 13 years. Laurie Murray died of cancer in 2009 after a long and fruitless search of her missing daughter. The Murray family remains confident that one day they'll finally get the answers to all of their questions. Fred provided these powerful words that remind us how much love a father has for his daughter: *"I wake up. It takes just a few seconds and then it [her missing daughter] crosses mind.*" Julie Murray, one of Maura's older sisters, told Boston Globe, "*There's no answers. There's that constant churning of your brain like: Well, what if this happened, or what if that happened? [...] Was the timing absolutely perfect for someone to be there on the spot and snatch her up and do something bad to her? What are the chances of that?*" Her brother Fred, Jr. also added, "*There's so many things that could have happened. It's going to take someone coming forward with a piece of information to solve it and it's probably something simple. The likely scenario is that she got picked up by someone. Maura is very smart but she's not street smart. She grew up in Hanson, Massachusetts.*"

There are still numerous signs posted around eastern US of the missing adult. If anyone has any information regarding Maura Murray's whereabouts or have sighted her ever before, please contact the University of Massachusetts Police at 1-413-545-2121. Her family is looking for the one clue that can stitch together the series of half-understood evidence and paint a picture of the whole truth.

THE MISSING IRISH WOMEN

ANDREA TORRENCE

Ireland's Vanishing Triangle

Between March 1993 and July 1998, eight young women vanished from the face of the Earth. The disappearance of the women has been dubbed "Ireland's Vanishing Triangle" by the media. The women were all last seen in the Leinster Province in eastern Ireland and none of their bodies have ever been recovered. To date, the mysterious Vanishing Triangle still troubles the families of the young women, police investigators, conspiracy theorists, and all of the peoples of Ireland.

The people missing women in the Ireland's Vanishing Triangle case all had very specific similarities: they were young, ranging from their teenagers to around 40 years old; their disappearances were sudden and without any significant clues for police to track despite the several large scale searches by Irish police force (Gardaí Síochána); and they all went missing after in the same geographical location.

The name "Vanishing Triangle" refers to the triangular shape of the location in the eastern part of the island, all within the boundaries of the Leinster Province. The unofficial list for the missing women in the Vanishing Triangle consists of six women, but a total of eight women have been reported missing within the same time frame and location of the others. Some speculate that, because of the similarities and oddities of the eight women's disappearances, they all became victims to a serial killer who frequented the Leinster Province during that period.

The cases of the Vanishing Triangle are still often featured in Irish media from time to time, even after a two decade-long search for the victims. They have also become the subject in numerous documentaries about unsolved crimes, including the TV-3 production of "Disappeared in the Mountains" by a local Irish TV station. Operation Trace is an effort by the Guardaí to solve this case of eight missing persons but has yet to yield substantial results, despite the promise of a €10,000 reward for information that leads to the recovery of any of the eight women's bodies.

There are a total of eight missing women in the Ireland's Vanishing Triangle case. The terrifying disappearances began in 1993 with Annie McCarrick – a 26-year old from New York who was taking her undergraduate studies in Ireland. She chose to continue go to college in Ireland in order to reconnect with her country's history and family heritage. She lived in an apartment with two female roommates in Sandymount, a suburb located on the Southside of Dublin. In March 1993, Annie was excitedly waiting for her mother, Nancy McCarrick, to visit her in Ireland.

On Friday, March 26th, only a few days before her mother's arrival, Annie was expected to come to her office to collect her paycheck but she never came. Previously, Annie made dinner plans with her friend, Hilary Brady, and his girlfriend, Rita Fortune, at her apartment on Saturday, March 27th. Her friends found it odd that Annie, who had arranged the whole appointment, was not in her apartment and her roommates had no idea where she had gone to. They immediately contacted Annie's parents in New York to inform them of their missing daughter.

Her father, John McCarrick, immediately had the feeling that something was wrong. "She was always reaching out and touching someone," he told reporters in an interview. "She would never have gone a day without talking to someone. We were very, very concerned." Both Nancy and John immediately boarded a plane to Ireland where they could help in the hunt for their missing daughter. The search for Annie became one of Ireland's largest wide scale searches for a missing person in the country's history.

Testimonies from witnesses place Annie in a local bank and grocery store on the morning of her disappearance. Another witness said that Annie was on a No. 44 city bus headed towards the small village of Enniskerry. The night of her disappearance, several pub-goers recalled seeing Annie at Johnny's Pub, located three miles past the borders of Enniskerry and at the foot of the Wicklow Mountains. The terrifying thing about this testimony is that witnesses said that she was accompanied by an unknown man. At the time, nobody was aware of Annie being involved in a relationship with a man so the Gardaí had no leads or suspects. After six months of fruitless searching, Nancy and John returned to the United States.

This was just the beginning of the Vanishing Triangle case of missing women in Leinster Province in Ireland. Just 3 months after Annie's disappearance, the family of Eva Brennan would receive the same heart-shattering news of a missing loved one. Corlette, Eva's sister, told reporters, "I remember seeing [Annie's] father on the television in Ireland and remember seeing the sorrow and the sadness and the anguish on that family's face... I couldn't imagine anybody going through that. But it was a very short 12 weeks later that [our family] were going through the exact same thing with Eva."

Eva Brennan, aged 39 at the time of her disappearance, was a local of Rathgar, Dublin. She went missing on July 25, 1993, only several months after Annie McCarrick. Eva's family recall her being extremely depressed after departing from a family lunch at her parents' home in Rathgar. Her father, Davy, went to her apartments after not receiving any news from his daughter for two days. After ringing her doorbell several times to no avail, he asked the barman at his family-owned pub, the Horse and Hound Pub, to assist him in breaking a window at Eva's apartment in order to enter the premises. Upon entering, Davy remembered seeing the jacket that she had worn to the family lunch.

After reporting their missing daughter to the Gardaí, their case was put on hold for a whole three months before any official investigation was launched. The family has openly criticized the Gardaí for mishandling Eva's disappearance. Similar to the search for Annie McCarrick, the police found no substantial evidence of where Eva would disappear to and why. Rumors circulated and were reported by some members of the Irish Police Force that Eva was an acquaintance of the infamous double-killer Michael Bambrick who was convicted of killing and hiding the bodies of Patricia McGauley and Mary Cummins in Clondalkin, Dublin.

Corlette expressed her doubt that she even knew Bambrick. She further stated that nobody had ever known of Eva stepping foor into Clondalkin, Dublin, or the southern city where Bambrick originated from. Corlette mentioned that Eva would visit her parents' home every day, would have lunch with them, and then retire to her apartment. Eva was not one to go out and socialize with others, let alone get close with a person who was well-known for murdering two women.

A full five months would pass before another woman was added to the growing list of missing people in the Vanishing Triangle case. On January 3, 1994, Imelda Keenan, a 22-year old native from Mountmellick, vanished in the city of Waterford. She was registered as a student taking computer courses at Central Technical Institute at the time of her disappearance. Initially, Imelda went to stay with one of her brothers living in Cobh, County Cork. After a brief visit, she departed for Waterford where she would spend a couple nights with two other brothers. At the time of her disappearance, Imelda was sharing an apartment with her boyfriend, Mark Wall, in on William Street in Waterford.

On the day of her disappearance, Imelda told Mark that she was going to the post office to run some errands. She left their apartment at around 1:30 PM and she walked down William Street onto Lombard Street. Imelda was sighted whilst she was crossing the road by a local doctor's secretary with whom she was well acquainted with. The secretary and a friend saw Imelda crossing the road near the Tower Hotel. That was the last time Imelda was ever seen or heard from again.

A Garda search for Imelda was soon conducted but produced nothing. The search for the Central Technical Institute by her family and friends has been going on for over 20 years, and the €10,000 reward for information leading to the discover of Imelda's whereabouts remains unclaimed. Her mother Elizabeth passed away in 2008 before finding getting closure on her missing daughter's case. "I don't think mammy could rest in peace," Imelda's brother Donal told reporters through tears. "Every mother likes to know where her baby is. That's what we want to know, we need our sister." Donal broke down and got onto his hands and knees during a gravesite ceremony in County Laois, begging for the return of their missing sister.

Donal added, "We are not looking for justice for Imelda. We are looking for Imelda. We do not wish for anyone to be held [accountable] for what may or may not have happened to [her]. We just want Imelda." He let the public know that the family will not charge any suspect for whatever misfortune has happened to his sister. "Closure for you and closure for the Keenan family is what's at stake."

After one year and ten months since Imelda disappeared, Josephine "JoJo" Dollard went missing on November 9, 1995. JoJo, 21-years old at the time, lived with a sister in a small village in County Kilkenny. She was raised by her older sisters who constantly worried for JoJo when she left the quiet town of Kilkenny to pursuit a career as a beautician in Dublin. On the date of her disappearance, she met with some friends in Dublin. She was supposed to take a bus and arrive at Kilkenny that evening, but she the time slipped her mind whilst chatting with friends and she ended up missing the bus for her return trip home. JoJo decided to hitchhike her way back to Kilkenny which was a common mode of transport for women in Ireland during that period.

Geraldine Niland – a journalist who wrote books on cases of missing women in Ireland – wrote the story of JoJo's return trip back to Kilkenny based on the testimonies of people who contacted her moments before her disappearance. After deciding to hitchhike home, Geraldine wrote that "Her first ride took her halfway to the little town of Moone. She phoned a friend from a phone box there, and told [her] that she was hitching a ride and waiting for another ride to come along." As she was talking to her friend, JoJo ended their conversation abruptly. "When [JoJo] was talking with her friend, she said, 'Oh, a car is coming, and I have to go now.' And she put the phone down. And that is the last we heard of Jojo Dollard."

Mary Phelan, one of JoJo's older sister and caregiver, remembered a brief conversation they had before JoJo's decision to move to the big city. "I gave her a little ring and a little bracelet," she says and she reminisces about her baby sister, "and I'll always remember in the room, she says to me, 'Mary, when I finish my beauty course in Dublin, I'll come home to you and I'll do your hair and I'll have you looking nice.' And I never saw her again. It's terrible."

Mary has done everything in her power to put pressure on the authorities to keep JoJo's case alive. She was inspired by the incredible story of a father who was in her exact same position: John McCarrick, father of Annie McCarrick. "I admired her dad," Mary told reporters about her initial response to seeing John on the television. "I thought, 'My God, what is that man going through? What is he really going through? [...] If John can go out there and do so much for Annie, then why can't I do it [for JoJo]? He was a great influence on me."

The next victim of Ireland's Vanishing Triangle was Fiona Pender. Fiona was added to the growing list of missing people in August 24, 1996, after her family reported to the authorities that their daughter's whereabouts were unknown. Fiona, 25-years old at the time and a native from Tullamore, County Offaly, was last seen by her boyfriend, John Thompson, as she was leaving her apartment building. The part-time model was seven months pregnant at the time of her disappearance. She reportedly went shopping for baby clothes the previous day.

The weeks following the initial report of Fiona's disappearance were filled with fruitless searching in local bogs, forests and rivers. Even the four-mile long Royal Canal was drained as investigators became desperate to find Fiona. A year after her disappearance, the police arrested five people and interrogated them about Fiona's whereabouts but were subsequently released without charge.

Not much information is available regarding the days prior to her disappearance. However, unlike the other women mentioned previously in this article, recent findings by the Gardaí have led to believe that Fiona died not long after vanishing. A suspect's wife came forward in 2014 with vital information that led to the arrest of her husband who she thinks murdered Fiona in 1996. The wife was allegedly assaulted by her husband who then told her that he would do "what [he] did to Fiona." The wife is currently in protective custody abroad.

The husband, now in his 40s, was captured abroad and charged with battery. Upon capture, the authorities received information that the body of Fiona could be found buried beneath a piece of farmland nearby Tullamore.

On February 13, 1997, Ciara Breen became the next missing person to be added to the names of missing women in the Ireland's Vanishing Tirangle case. Ciara was 18 years old at the time of her disappearance, and she was last seen by her mother Bernadette who said that they had just retired to their bedrooms after midnight. Bernadette got up at around 2 AM to use the bathroom and discovered that Ciara was not in her room. Her window was left open, and it is believed that Ciara did this intentionally to return back to her room after sneaking out. Authorities believe that she left her room to meet with an unknown person in the middle of the night, but no evidence points in that direction.

Since she disappeared, there have been two credible sightings of Ciara on the night she vanished. In 2015, Liam Mullen was taken into police custody following a lead that he was involved in Ciara's disappearance, but was soon released without being charged. He soon became the chief suspect in Ciara's case and was arrested again in 2017 following a suspicion of drunk driving. Before being under arrest, Mullen swallowed a substance that caused him to become ill. The on-call doctor at the Garda station was summoned to attend to the unconscious man, but despite their efforts to resuscitate the dying man, Mullen silently passed away and was pronounced dead on the spot. There was no proof that states the police had mishandled the man in any way.

Friends of Ciara told the authorities that Mullen had approached them on the day before she went missing. The friends overheard their plans to rendezvous the following night. Mullen denied ever having the conversation with Ciara, and although lands belonging to Mullen and his family were searched, the police did not find any conclusive evidence of his involvement in Ciara's missing persons case until his 2017 arrest.

Fiona Sinnott, 19-years old at the time and a native of Rosslare, County Wexford, was went missing on February 9, 1989. She was currently residing in Broadway during that period. Reports say that on February 8th, Sinnott had just left a pub with Sean Carroll – her ex-boyfriend and father of their 11-month old daughter. While being interrogated by investigators, Carroll said that he escorted Sinnott back to her home in Bayhitt, and added that he spent the night on her couch.

That night, Sinnott had been complaining about arm and upper body pains and decided to go straight to bed. On the morning of her disappearance, Caroll allegedly walked into Sinnott's room and found her wide awake. She told him that she was still experiencing pain and was planning on hitchhiking to the hospital later that day. Carroll reportedly gave her £3 for the trip and left her house. He was picked up by his mother who drove him back to their family home where their 11-month old daughter was staying at the time. This was the last time anyone had seen or heard from Sinnott for the last 20 years.

Investigations by the police found that Sinnott had not met with a doctor that day since there were no medical records of her visit or any scheduled surgeries. The authorities failed to produce evidence that she had even attempted to hitchhike to the hospital. While investigating in her house, the Gardaí found that it had been emptied of many of her personal possessions. Alan Bailey, a retired detective who was tasked with investigating Sinnott's disappearance, told reporters that, "There was a complete absence of clothing and other personal items indicating that a teenage girl and her 11-month old daughter were actually living there."

News of Sinnott's disappearance spread, and a local farmer informed the Gardaí that he discovered several black garbage bags in the corner of his fields. The contents of the bags were documents and items with Sinnott's name written on them. The farmer initially set the bags on fire as he thought they were just evidence of illegal dumping.

It wasn't until February 18th, a full nine days after her disappearing, that she was reported missing to the authorities. Fiona's father, Pat, alerted the police of the situation when he contacted the Kimore Garda Station. He informed them that his daughter had not been sighted since the 8th. The Gardaí responded with a full-scale investigation of a missing persons.

The Gardaí have treated this case as a murder investigation and believe that the suspect behind Sinnott's disappearance is a person who as well acquainted with her. The police searched lakes and body dump sites but have returned empty handed. Within the first few weeks of the investigation, one witness told police that they had heard a woman's scream in the Millpond Cross area on the same night Fiona reportedly left the pub with Carroll. Another witness, a passing motorist, reported seeing a couple on the side of the road who were in a heated argument. Neither reports had been proven nor linked back to Sinnott's case.

Many people believe that Wexford residents are trying their best to cover up what happened to Sinnott. Rumors have surfaced that the locals were actively involved in concealing her murder and burial site. Other reports show that the locals are intimidated by the suspect and would do anything in their power to not cross him. In 2008, a memorial plaque dedicated to Sinnott's memory was stolen from a cemetery in Wexford. The plaque, previously cemented to the wall, was stolen on the night before it was to be unveiled to the public.

The last person to be added to the list of missing women in the Vanishing Triangle case was Deirdre Jacob. This 18-year old native of Newbridge, County Kildare, was reported missing on July 28, 1998. She was staying in Twickenham, London, and taking her undergraduate studies at St. Mary's University. At the time of her disappearance, Deirdre was back in Ireland for summer break.

On the afternoon of her disappearance, Deirdre was running errands on Newbridge's high street when she visited a bank, the post office, and made a quick stop to her grandmother's newspaper and magazine shop across the road before walking home. She was just several yards from her parents' home (according to testimonies by passing motorists and pedestrians) but never made it to her front door.

Two months after her she went missing, the Gardaí found a link between her case and five other cases of missing women in the previous years. Operation Trace was launched to investigate the similarities between the cases. The other victims allegedly connected to the missing persons case of Deirdre include Annie McCarrick, JoJo Dollard, Fiona Pender, Ciara Breen, and Fiona Sinnott.

Deirdre's parents, Michael and Bernadette Jacobs, have repeatedly criticized the Gardaí for their lack of interest in their daughter's case and their sluggish progress in uncovering new information and following new leads. Although the case has gone cold over the past several years, rumors and new pieces of information regularly surface. They are aware of the various assumptions and theories surrounding their missing daughter's case. One of the most believed theories is Larry Murphy raping and murdering their daughter and several other missing women.

Larry Murphy, a convicted rapist and attempted murderer, was imprisoned for 15 years beginning in 2000. Subsequent to his arrest, Murphy became the suspect of many of the women's disappearance cases in the Vanishing Triangle. In 2000, he was charged with rape and attempted murder on an unnamed woman who was bound by Murphy and driven roughly 40 kilometers away into a remote area in a forest. He raped her four times and tried to strangle her to death before he was unintentionally thwarted by passing deer hunters. The hunters' car's headlights momentarily stunned the man, allowing his victim to flee and run towards their direction. They brought her to the closest police station where she testified that Murphy had committed the awful atrocities against her. He was arrested and tried in court before being sentenced to 15 years for rape and attempted murder. During his incarceration, there appeared to be a complete cease to young women disappearing in the Leinster area.

However, Michael and Bernadette remain unconvinced that Murphy was even involved in the case, despite the public's and police's strong belief that he put an end to their daughter's life. "We need people to refocus without the shadows of Larry Murphy," Michael told reporters.

From between 2000 and 2012, no substantial information was discovered or offered to the Gardaí, and most of the missing women's cases soon went cold. Larry Murphy was in jail and this supposedly put an end to all the disappearances and murders. However, in late October 2012, the people of Ireland found a renewed interest in the Vanishing Triangle case following the abduction and murder of a pregnant 30-year old native of Couny Laois. The woman, Aoife Phelan, disappeared as she was heading home from a friend's house. The remains of her body were found, and a 24-year old man named Robert Corbet was charged with murder. He as supposedly the father of her unborn child, and they had gotten into an argument in his home before murdering her. In 2014, he was sentenced to spend the remainder of his life behind bars.

To date, there are still posters and coverage on TV and radio regarding the Ireland's Vanishing Triangle cases. It's difficult for a country of that size to soon forget the terrible horrors that plagued its citizens for roughly six years. "People remember their names to this day," says Alan Bailey who helmed the Gardaí taskforce in charge of finding a link between the eight missing women, "because they went missing of a short time period in a certain part of the country and because they were normal people going about their everyday routine." Alan gave his opinion on the whole Vanishing Triangle ordeal to reporters, stating that, "The Deirdre Jacob case was particularly troubling because she disappeared in broad daylight during the afternoon and close to her home in Newbridge."

The unexplainable disappearances of several women in a short period of time could have been attributed to the lack of surveillance cameras. Alan spoke of the matter, saying, "In the case of Annie McCarrick, the only CCTV footage we have of her on the day she disappeared was in her local bank." If Annie were to disappear during this time and age of technology and public surveillance, then the authorities would have more information and be "far better placed to trace her movements."

The families of the victims show no signs of wanting to give up on their 20-year long search for their loved ones. If anybody has any information regarding the whereabouts of any of these women, please contact the Irish Police Force or members of their families.